PARANORMAL
FAMILY AND
FRIENDS

PARANORMAL
FAMILY AND
FRIENDS

FRANK R. SANTARIGA

iUniverse, Inc.
Bloomington

Paranormal Family and Friends

iUniverse books may be ordered through booksellers or by contacting:

iUniverse
1663 Liberty Drive
Bloomington, IN 47403
www.iuniverse.com
1-800-Authors (1-800-288-4677)

ISBN: 978-1-4620-4502-0 (sc)
ISBN: 978-1-4620-4504-4 (hc)
ISBN: 978-1-4620-4503-7 (ebk)

Printed in the United States of America

iUniverse rev. date: 08/26/2011

Contents

Part II: Paranormal Friends

Acknowledgments

I would like to thank my family and friends for sharing their personal experiences. Their encouragement and support made the writing of *Paranormal Family and Friends* a true pleasure and a rewarding endeavor.

Thanks again, everyone.

Introduction

The accounts described in *Paranormal Family and Friends* are among the best that I have investigated and researched in my twenty-five years as a parapsychologist (a person who researches and investigates the supernatural, such as ghosts, spirits, UFOs, and other activities or events that are not easily explained through traditional scientific methods). What makes these events even more remarkable is that I personally know the people who recounted the incidents and can vouch for their character. In the cases where people are retelling experiences of their close friends or relatives, they too, unconditionally vouch for the integrity of the storyteller.

Keep in mind that the experiences you will read about did not occur only to people who possessed psychic abilities; for the most part, they occurred to people just like you and me.

You will read of my mother's visions, which to this day continue to plague her; join my father and his friend on a fishing trip where they catch more than fish; and experience the ghostly incidents, UFOs, and other strange encounters that changed the lives of my brother, aunts, cousins, and friends.

In most instances, the actual names of the people depicted in the account were used. However, there are instances where fictitious names were required to protect the privacy of other participants.

In writing *Paranormal Family and Friends,* I wanted to reveal to the curious and to the followers of the paranormal that you do not have to look very far to find people who have had paranormal experiences. You need only to ask your family and friends.

My goal was to make *Paranormal Family and Friends* an effortless and amusing read. It wouldn't surprise me if you finish reading it in just a sitting or two. However long it takes, I hope you enjoy the experience as much as I have enjoyed bringing it to you.

Just remember this one thing as you read each story: it really did happen!

Part 1

Paranormal Family

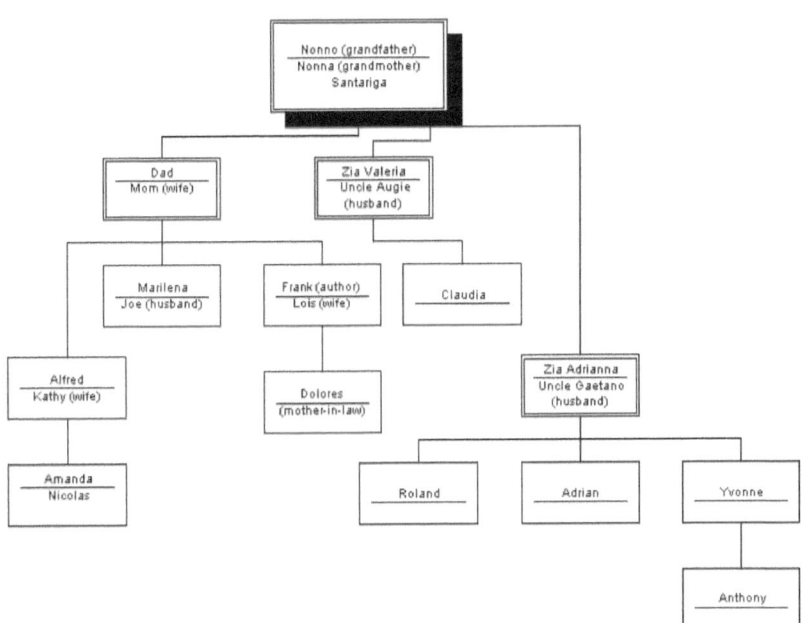

Mom's Visions

The following accounts were given to me by my mother, Bruna Santariga. My mother has had psychic abilities as long as I can remember. Unfortunately, these events are usually are preceded by a major migraine headache; soon after, she has these "visions," which seem to result in ominous occurrences.

The Apparition of Adrian

My cousin Adrian died suddenly at the age of twenty-six. At the time of her passing, I was living in Colorado, but I was told the following incident upon my return to New York, during a family gathering. Knowing of my involvement in the paranormal, my family was anxious to hear my opinion regarding the strange occurrences surrounding Adrian's death.

The morning of February 22, 1974, started like most midwinter days in my hometown of Yonkers, New York. The sky was bright and sunny, and the snow was on the ground from the previous weekend's storm. As my mother was getting ready for work, she complained about waking up with a headache. For my mother, this was nothing new. As far back as I could remember she had always suffered from chronic high blood pressure, which caused her numerous headaches. However, this time it was more than just another headache; she also had an accompanying uneasy feeling that was causing her a peculiar anxiety.

Shrugging it off, Mom packed her lunch, bundled herself up and made her way down New Main Street to the dress shop where she worked as a dressmaker.

As the morning moved on, her headache somewhat diminished, but in contrast, the queasy feeling seemed to be growing. Looking at the clock, she noticed that it was almost 10:30 a.m. and thought that perhaps having some lunch and taking aspirin would help relieve her symptoms.

Running out of material, my mother leaned over and reached into a bin for more fabric. When she pulled up a bulk of the fabric, Mom jolted back in shock as she was suddenly gripped by a ghastly vision. She had uncovered what seemed to be a head and upper torso of a person.

At first, my mother could not identify the figure, but slowly it came into focus. Totally traumatized, she recognized the person: it was my cousin Adrian.

As soon as Mom recognized the figure to be Adrian, she became light-headed and fainted. Everyone ran over to help her. One of the men who worked there gave her some water. He then asked if she would like to see a doctor or go home. My mother thanked him but said she was fine and solemnly went back to work. To her surprise, the creepy feeling that had plagued her all morning had disappeared.

Mom had just finished lunch and was getting back to work when my dad walked into the shop. He walked over to my mother, but before he could speak, she asked, "What are you doing here? Shouldn't you be at work?"

My father was about to give the reason why he was there when my mother abruptly stopped him and said, "Wait, don't tell me, I know why you are here. You're here to tell me that Adrian is dead."

Dad stepped back, not believing what he had just heard. He asked Mom, "How did you know?"

Mom told him about the troubling feeling she had had since waking up that morning and about the vision that had appeared to her.

My father explained that my cousin Yvonne, Adrian's older sister, knowing that Adrian had not been feeling well, had been trying to reach her that morning. Not being able reach her by phone, Yvonne asked Adrian's boyfriend, Gary, to go to her apartment to see if everything was okay. When Gary got there, he found Adrian in bed and not breathing. He immediately called 911. The EMS people came quickly, but it was to no avail. Adrian did not respond to any of their procedures, and she was finally pronounced dead at ten thirty that morning.

A couple of days later, my mother and father went to the funeral home for the wake. As they approached the casket, my mother started to shake and told my father to hold on to her arm and quickly find a place to sit. My father noticed my mother was very upset and asked what was wrong. My mother told him that Adrian was wearing the exact dress that my mother had seen on the day of her vision.

Mary Balboa's Strange Good-Bye

The next incident again reveals my mother's psychic ability. It is one of the few times that Mom did not get a headache before one of her paranormal experiences.

For many years my mother would spend most of the winters with my sister Marilena and her family in Florida, and the winter of 1997–1998 was no different—or so she thought. At about the same time, a friend of the family, Mary Balboa, was also heading to Florida. Mary was going to visit her sister. Mary and her sister had had their share of disagreements throughout the years. Mary had a serious illness and was confined to a wheelchair, and she wanted to make sure there were no hard feelings between her and her sister if, God forbid, something should happen to her. Knowing that my mother would be in Florida too, Mary called Mom to tell her she would stop by and visit her and Marilena.

Well, things did not go as planned for Mary. It seemed that everything thing she said or did caused the two sisters to argue. Mary was very upset, and she asked her sister if she could please take her to Marilena's so she could visit with my mother. Being very spiteful, Mary's sister ignored her request.

Meanwhile, my mother, not hearing from Mary, assumed that Mary and her sister were busy and that Mary would probably get in touch with her later. Little did my mother know the difficulty Mary was experiencing during the visit.

My cousin Yvonne and Mary were best friends, and not hearing from Mary troubled Yvonne. When Yvonne finally got in touch with Mary, she asked, "How are you and your sister getting along?" Mary told Yvonne about the arguing and fighting. Crying, Mary said that she was not feeling well and that she was planning to go home within a couple of days.

My mother did not know the trouble Mary was having with her sister. Although she was wondering why she had not heard from Mary, it did not concern her that much. That is, until one night.

My mother had gone to bed, but she was having a hard time falling asleep. She did not like the feeling she was experiencing—the kind of feeling that always accompanied bad news.

Noticing that it was almost 11:00 p.m., my mother rolled onto her side, trying to get comfortable. She saw what seemed to be smoke forming in midair. The substance became more detailed as my mother watched intensely. In just seconds, the wisp had transformed itself into the face of a person. Then the face of the person became very clear: it was the face of Mary Balboa.

Staring at the apparition of Mary, my mother heard her distinctly say, "Hello."

My mother, completely surprised, answered, "Hello."

With that, Mary smiled and slowly faded away.

The next morning, not mentioning anything to my sister about what had occurred the previous night, my mother sat down for breakfast. She started some small talk by asking my sister's kids if they were all ready for school. At that moment, the telephone rang. It was my cousin Yvonne; she had just gotten off the phone with Mary Balboa's sister. Mary's sister had wanted to let her know that Mary had passed away during the night.

My mother asked Yvonne, "Did she say what time it occurred?"

Yvonne answered, "I think Mary's sister mentioned it was about eleven o'clock last night."

My mother did not say anything to anyone about what she had seen that night.

Upon my mother's return from Florida, my aunts and Yvonne stopped by to visit with her. When the discussion of what happened to Mary Balboa came up, Yvonne said, "It was sad how Mary's life ended with her and her sister not getting along. And it was too bad she couldn't get to see you, Aunt Bruna, when you were at Marilena's."

My mother slowly looked up from the table and said to Yvonne, "Do you remember when you called to tell me about Mary? I asked you what time Mary died, and you said about 11:00 p.m."

My cousin answered, "Yes, I remember. Why?"

My mother went on to say, "At that same time, I saw an apparition of Mary's face; she said 'Hello' to me and then vanished."

I asked Yvonne what she thought of Mom's experience.

Her answer: "Knowing your mother, it didn't surprise me."

To this day, my mother continues to have paranormal experiences, but she very rarely talks about them.

Dad and Angelo's Encounter

This next account happens to be my favorite for two reasons: First, it involves my dad and his best friend, Angelo. And second, you could not find a more skeptical pair of people in the world.

Revenge of Hanged Man's Ghost

It started one summer afternoon in 1975. I was at my parents' house, having lunch and discussing my new job in Connecticut, when my father's best friend and old army buddy, Angelo, walked in. Angelo said he was in the neighborhood and had dropped by to say hello. Surprised to see me there, he came over and sat down.

He put his arm around me and started hitting me with all kinds of questions. "How the heck are you? I haven't seen you in years. Are you back from Colorado for good? Your dad told me you're still going to school. What are you studying now?"

In my family, the running joke was that I had been going to school all my life, so when people would see me, they would ask, "How are you?" immediately followed by, "So what are going to school for now?"

I told Angelo, "I've received my certification in parapsychology and have started investigating and doing research in the tri-state area."

Angelo had a puzzled expression on his face. "Parapsychology, what the hell is that?" he asked.

I explained to Angelo that parapsychology is the study of psychic phenomena. "We investigate reports of supernatural experiences, ghosts or spirits, UFOs, and other activities or events that are not easily explained through traditional scientific methods."

Then, as if I had said something unspeakable, Angelo asked in a very low voice, "Did your father ever tell you what happened to us the last time we went fishing at Montauk?"

My father spoke up and said, "You're not going to tell him about that crap, are you?"

Angelo said, "Hell, yeah. Maybe he can tell us what we saw."

With that comment, Dad got up from the table in a huff, lit a cigarette, and went out onto the patio.

During WWII, Angelo and my father had served in the US Army and had seen action in North Africa, Italy, and Germany. Unfortunately, both had seen more than their share of death and destruction. Yet, because of that that, I would not think that anything they could experience could ever "spook" them.

The point I am trying to make is you will never find two more straight shooters than these guys. The word "skeptic" is too mellow to describe them, especially my dad.

My curiosity now had the better of me, and I could not wait to hear what had happened to Angelo and my dad.

The Frightening Fishing Trip

At least once every winter, Angelo and my dad went to Montauk Point, Long Island, New York, to fish for whiting. Whiting are small codfish that are abundant during cold weather, especially at Montauk. Montauk Point is about 120 miles east of New York City on Long Island. From my father's house in Yonkers, New York, it is probably about 140 miles. In all, it is about a three- to four-hour ride, depending on traffic and weather.

What Angelo told me that day had happened on the night of Washington's birthday, in February 1973.

There was hardly any traffic, the weather was clear and cold, and the trip to Montauk took them a little over three hours. The road leading to their favorite parking spot in front of the old abandoned Coast Guard base had not been maintained since the base was closed back in the early 1950s. There was no way they could take their car any closer to their fishing spot. It was just a few minutes before 9:00 p.m. when they arrived outside the entrance to the old Coast Guard base.

They gathered up their gear and started their quarter-mile walk to their favorite fishing spot. On the way, they passed the old airplane hangar, some rusted-out cars, rolls of wire cables, and all kinds of old junk.

They finally arrived at their favorite spot on the pier. It was the perfect night for catching whiting: the tide was high, the temperature was just right (cold), and there were a million stars in the sky. Now all they had to do was fill the two five-gallon buckets with whiting!

Luck was on their side that night, or so it seemed. They filled both buckets in less than two hours and were ready to head back home. My dad packed away the lantern, portable heater, blankets, and camping chairs. Angelo took the hooks off the fishing poles, reeled in the excess line, locked the spools, and put the lids on the two buckets of fish. Each of them lit cigarettes, and they headed toward the entrance of the base.

There they were, walking along the road with their catch. Angelo noted how eerily quiet it was. The only thing they heard was the crunching of the frozen snow under their feet. It was at this point that Angelo thought he saw a light coming from the abandoned airplane hangar.

He turned to my dad and asked him if he saw the light too.

My dad, with his cigarette dangling from his mouth, said, "Yeah, it's probably a bum trying to keep warm. Can't say I blame him."

Angelo was now keeping one eye on the hangar and the other on the snowy road. He did not like the creepy feeling he was getting. My father, on the other hand, was more concerned with getting to the car, putting everything away, and turning on the heater.

As they got closer to the hangar, Angelo noticed that the light from inside was getting more intense. It was as if with every step they took, the light became brighter.

Angelo called over to my father and said, "I think that bum is going to burn that hangar down; look how bright that fire's become."

Dad replied, "On the way home, we'll stop by the fire station and let them know about the fire."

They continued their brisk walk to the car. When they were about sixty feet from the hangar, Angelo and my father jumped as the hangar doors blew open. From inside the hangar, a wispy form started to float out. It almost looked like a small cloud, and it was gliding toward them.

With the wispy form no more than ten feet in front of them, they noticed that it was taking the shape of a person. Suddenly, out of nowhere, they heard a horrifying shriek, which broke the stillness of the dark cold night.

Angelo, in a panic, dropped all the gear and started running back toward the pier. My dad took off after him and caught him just before he reached the treacherous part of the pier that was missing planks.

Angelo, shocked and wide-eyed, turned to my dad and said, "Did you see that?"

My dad answered, nonchalant, "What are you talking about? That was only our imagination."

Angelo answered wildly, "Imagination, my ass."

They walked nervously back toward where they had dropped the gear and buckets of fish. As they got closer to the hangar, they started to get very uncomfortable and anxious. Almost directly in front of the hangar, they stopped and stared toward the doors. To their shock, the hangar doors were still padlocked, and there was no light coming from within.

That's when my dad said, "We need to get a coffee—real quick."

You Saw a Ghost

Visibly traumatized, my dad and Angelo headed for the all-night diner on Old Montauk Highway. They wasted no time getting to the diner; luckily, it was only a couple of miles from where they had been fishing.

Angelo, still shaking, was trying to take a sip of his coffee when the owner behind the counter said, "I didn't think it was that cold out there."

Angelo answered back, "It's not the cold that has me shaking like this."

Then before Angelo could say another word, the diner owner said, "Well, then, you must have seen Hanged Man's Ghost!"

Both my father and Angelo look at each other, stunned by what they had just heard.

Then Angelo asked, "How did you know?"

The owner replied, "You aren't the first guys to see Hanged Man's Ghost, hell no."

Angelo asked, "So, you're telling us that we saw a ghost?"

The diner owner answered with a story. "Well, this is the way I heard it. During WWII, the Coast Guard base was a very important base. One of the sailors stationed there had earned a three-day leave, and since it fell on Washington's birthday, he was able to add an extra day to it. The sailor lived in Queens, New York, which was only a few hours by train, and he decided he would surprise his wife, not calling her or telling or about his trip home."

The diner owner went on to say, "Well, you guessed it. When the sailor got home, he opened the door and didn't see his wife in the kitchen, and so he went into the bedroom, where he caught his wife in bed with another guy. In a rage, the sailor ran into the kitchen, grabbed a knife, killed the guy, and then killed his wife. Realizing what he had done, the sailor jumped on the next train back to Montauk. Once back on the base, he went into the storage room, grabbed a rope, and headed for the airplane hangar."

My father asked, "Didn't anyone see him doing this?"

The diner owner replied, "Well, from my understanding, it was pretty late, around midnight, when it all happened."

The diner owner poured Angelo and my dad another cup of coffee and continued his story. "So, the sailor made his way up to the rafters, put the rope around his neck, and jumped."

Angelo and my dad shook their heads, shocked and saddened by the terrible chain of events.

They both looked at the diner owner as he finished the story: "What they tell me is that every few years, always on Washington's birthday, the sailor remembers the hanging and runs out of the hangar screaming. So, gentlemen, congratulations! You two were lucky enough to see Hanged Man's Ghost tonight."

Angelo, after telling me about his experience, asked, "Do you think it really happened, or do you think someone was just pulling our chain?"

I answered, "Knowing both you and my dad, I definitely don't think it was your imaginations. I think you really witnessed what they call a 'residual haunting'; I think you really saw something very strange and unexplainable."

Angelo sat there, a little dumbfounded but relieved to get the story off his chest. Then we went out to the patio and joined my dad under the grapevine.

Our Investigation

A few weeks later, and without mentioning anything to my father, my friend Joe and I decided to spend a couple of days at Montauk. I figured we could take in a little fishing and a little ghost hunting all at the same time. We got there Saturday afternoon. It was raining, and so we decided that that day would be the best time to do our ghost hunting.

We had no trouble finding the old Coast Guard base. However, there was a ten-foot fence surrounding it. Joe and I got out of the car and started walking around to see if there was any way we could get in. We had not walked more than twenty feet when a police car came up slowly behind us. He flashed his lights, which we took to mean, "Stop there and wait for me to get out of the car."

The police officer walked up and asked if he could be of any help. I told him our names and asked if we could get onto the base and check out the old airplane hangar.

He was very polite and said, "The base is locked up and is off limits to the public. You need special permission from the US Coast Guard in order to enter it."

He went on to ask, "Why do you want to go into that hell hole, anyway?"

I told him that I was a parapsychologist and part of my research was to investigate and confirm the report of the base being haunted. He repeated himself, stating that we would need permission from the Coast Guard in order to enter the base.

Inquiring further, he asked, "What makes you think this place is haunted?"

I explained, "We heard reports from reliable witnesses who had strange experiences here some years back."

At that answer, the police officer shook his head and laughed. He said, "That was one of the reasons they had to lock this place up. People were coming in here looking for the ghost. A couple of them fell through the old pier and drowned!"

I asked, "So, then, it's true? The place is haunted?"

Again, he made a little laugh and said, "The only thing I know is what a former partner told me about this place."

I said, "What was that?"

He related the story his old partner had told.

"One night a few years back, my partner was making his tour around the roads by the base when something caught his eye coming from the old airplane hangar. It looked to him as if there was someone with a lantern walking around in the hangar. He pulled his car over and asked for backup before entering the hangar. While waiting for his backup, he kept an eye on the light in the hangar. He then heard the sound of a car coming from behind him. He turned and saw it was his backup coming down the road.

"His back was still turned, and he was looking at the patrol car coming toward him when he heard a horrific scream coming from the hangar behind him. He turned quickly and caught a glimpse of what he made out as a wisp of smoke floating through the air. The backup patrol car pulled alongside him, and the officer asked, 'What's up?'"

"My partner, not wanting the other patrolman to think he was crazy, answered, 'I thought I saw a light in the hangar and wanted backup here before going in.' They unlocked the gate and went in, but they couldn't find anything unusual. My partner never mentioned to the other police officer about the scream or the smokelike wisp that floated through the night air. After checking out the hangar, they locked the gate and left, making nothing further of the incident."

I asked, "What made your partner tell you about this?"

The police officer replied, "You know, I really don't know why he told me. Maybe because it was his last week on the force, and he just wanted to get it off his chest?"

I asked, "Do you believe this really happened to him?"

He was quick to answer, "Absolutely! I was his partner; we trusted each other with our lives!"

Then the policeman got back into his "officer" role and told us we couldn't park there and we needed to move on. With that, Joe and I decided to head for the diner on old Montauk Highway to see what we could find out there.

It took us about fifteen minutes to get to the diner. It was pouring rain as we rolled into the parking lot; however, we lucked out and found a parking space close to the entrance. Once we were inside, we took a couple of seats at the counter. I looked around and looked for the oldest person working there. I figured that if anyone had heard about Hanged Man's Ghost, it would be the most senior person. Seeing an older person cleaning a booth, I called him over.

He asked, "What would you gentlemen like?"

Both Joe and I ordered a hamburger, fries, and a Coke.

I then asked, "How long have you worked here?"

He answered, "Eight months."

Disappointed, I asked, "Is there anyone who has worked here longer than that, like maybe for a few years and heard of a story about Hanged Man's Ghost?"

He said, "Yes, him. There." He then pointed to a younger man—whom I would have picked as the newest member to join their team.

Joe said, "Let me go over and ask if he knows anything about this Hanged Man's Ghost you're looking for."

I saw the man and Joe talking, shaking their heads in agreement, and then Joe headed back to the counter. Joe told me that the guy knew about the Hanged Man's Ghost and was willing to talk to us on his break, which was in ten minutes. In the meantime, we ate our meals and enjoyed watching the rain from the dry diner.

The Validation

The fellow came over as promised and asked if we didn't mind sitting in the smoking section so he could have a cigarette during his break. We told him that was not a problem, so we headed for a booth at the back of the diner. The fellow introduced himself as Jeff and said that he had lived in Montauk all his life and was very familiar with Hanged Man's Ghost story.

I asked, "What can you tell us about it?"

Here's what he told us: "I have never had an unusual experience back when we were able to get onto the base. However, some of my friends supposedly heard moans or cries when they entered the hangar. Nevertheless, the event that stands out the most in my mind happened right here in the diner, about three years ago when the original owner still had the place. At that time, I was only working part time—after school and on the weekends. I can remember it as if it happened last night. It was a little after one in the morning, and a man came into the diner all wide-eyed and shouting loudly for the owner to call the cops. He believed that someone was being murdered down the road.

"There was just the owner, the cook, and me in the diner at the time, and when we heard the racket, all of us came running out to see what was wrong. The guy was clearly out of his mind. He grabbed the shirt collar of the cook and kept repeating, 'Call the cops! Call the cops!'

"The owner stepped in and said, 'Wait a minute, you need to calm down so we can understand what's wrong.' The guy sank onto the bench of one of the booths and then looked up and insisted that we call the police. The owner told me to call the station house and have them send over Joey, who was the officer who usually patrolled our area.

"As I was making the call, the guy started to tell us his story. He worked the second shift at a factory in the area, and he had been driving home from work. He passed by the old base to see if anyone he knew was fishing. He had pulled the car alongside of the hangar and was looking toward the pier, when from behind him he heard this dreadful scream. Looking over his shoulder, he thought he saw someone run into the hangar, but—here's the kicker—the hangar doors were closed and locked.

"Just as he was finishing telling us about this strange occurrence, Joey, the patrolman, walked in the door and asked what the problem was. The owner of the diner grabbed Joey by the arm and walked away from us, speaking to him very softly. As they were talking at the other end of the diner, the cook gave the guy a cup of coffee and assured him that the police officer would look into the incident. The man had somewhat calmed down and took a sip of his coffee. Another customer came in, and I went over to take care of him.

"While I was waiting on the second customer, I saw the patrolman and the diner owner talking to the man, and then about a minute later, the man and the patrolman walked out of the diner together. I don't know where they went, but they both got into the patrol car and left. I went over and asked the owner, 'What do you think happened?'

"He looked at me and said, 'It's that damn Hanged Man's Ghost playing tricks again.'"

"I asked, 'So you think it was the ghost that scared him?'"

"The owner answered, 'What else could it have been?'"

Our storyteller added one last thought: "That's my experience with Hanged Man's Ghost. Like I said before, as many times as I have been at the base, I personally have never heard or seen anything strange."

With that bit of information, Joe and I thanked the young man and headed to our motel. We passed the Coast Guard base one more time. We did not say a word, but we both wondered if Hanged Man's Ghost still roamed the rusty hangar in search of absolution for his crime. I guess we'll never know.

Alfred's Experiences

My brother Alfred is sixteen years my junior, so I do not recall much from the years he was growing up. By the time Al was six, I was married and out of the house. I really began to know my brother when I returned from Colorado and went to live with my folks again. I found I was no longer looking down to speak with him; I was stretching my neck and looking up.

Anyhow, my brother and his wife, Kathy, live just outside of Poughkeepsie, New York, in a little town called LaGrange. They have two kids: a daughter, Amanda, who is sixteen, and a son, Nicholas, who is twelve.

When Al heard I was writing a book on the paranormal, he asked me, "Do you want to include some of my strange experiences?"

I said, "It depends; let's hear what they are."

Boy was I in for a surprise. I will list them in the order in which they occurred. Here is Al's first experience with the paranormal.

The Skunk Ape

It was the summer of 1974. Al and his cousin Anthony were spending the summer with my sister Marilena and her family in their new home in Davies, Florida. Just about every year, Al and Anthony spent the summer swimming in my sister's pool and helping her and her husband, Joe, around the house and sometimes at their restaurant.

One July night, Al and Anthony were watching TV while Joe, Marilena, and my sister's kids were sleeping. As they were watching TV, they noticed a very pungent odor coming from the back woods.

19

Al and Anthony wondered if a family of skunks was close by. They closed the windows and turned on the air conditioner in the room. Even with the air conditioner on, the stench was horrible.

The next morning, when they were having breakfast, Al mentioned to Marilena, "I think there's a family of skunks living in the back woods. Last night the smell was so bad we had to close the windows and turn on the air conditioner in order to watch TV."

Marilena responded, "I noticed that too. I guess the neighbors were right about the skunk ape coming by again."

Well, that caught the boys' attention. Almost simultaneously, they asked, "What are you talking about—a skunk ape?"

My sister explained, "When we first looked at the property, we decided to check out the neighbors. Since the property is pretty much out in the boondocks, the closest neighbors are almost a quarter of a mile down the road, and Joe and I wanted to be sure they would be the kind of people we would like to have close by."

My sister continued, "We stopped by the neighbor to introduce ourselves and said that we were interested in the property down the road and were checking out the area. The people were friendly and seemed happy that they were finally going to have someone living close by. In talking, Joe and I found out that they owned a small horse farm, and they just loved living there, except when the skunk ape came around."

"At that point, Joe asked, 'What's this skunk ape you're talking about?' The neighbor described a creature about seven to nine feet tall that looked like a man covered with hair and stunk to high heaven. Joe and I didn't know what to think, and so we smiled and thanked them for their time and headed back to take one last look at the property."

Al asked, "Weren't you curious about what they told you?"

My sister answered, "Not at the time. However, once we built the house and moved in, we did start to notice an awful smell coming from the woods every so often, mostly at night. Sometimes, you would hear a shrieking sound coming from the back woods, and it would scare the heck out of us."

She continued, "One day, I went back to our neighbor and told him about our experiences. He told me that the skunk ape had been living in these swamps and woods for hundreds of years. The Seminole Indians talked about the creature way back before Columbus's time. The neighbor went on to say that most of the time the creature stayed away from people. He mostly fed on plants and fish. However, they were known to eat farm animals when their food source was scarce."

Chuckling, Anthony said, "I think you're kidding us. You just don't want us to go roaming in the woods, and you're telling this story to scare us."

Marilena answered, "Hey, I'm just telling you what they told me. You can believe it or not."

Al chimed in, "If that thing is so big, it would leave tracks all over the place."

Marilena answered, "And it does! Joe has seen them a few times when he dumps the lawn cuttings back there."

Hearing that, both Al and Anthony decided to go to the woods to see if they could spot any tracks.

They wanted to prove to Marilena and to themselves that there was no such thing as a skunk ape.

Signs of the Skunk Ape

After finishing their breakfast and chores, Al and Anthony went out the kitchen door and into the heat and humidity of a typical Florida summer day. Even though it was still morning, they could feel the sweat pouring down. Standing on the deck, the boys began to scan the woods. Shading their eyes from the blinding sun, they noticed an area of trampled tall weeds. They summoned their courage and made their way toward the spot.

As they approached the flattened patch, they started to smell the same nauseating odor they had experienced the night before. The odor increased as they got closer to the crushed weeds. Standing in front of the spot, they could make out what looked to be tracks heading deeper into the swamp area of the woods. Then, no more than a few feet from where they were standing, they distinctly saw a number of huge tracks in the mud.

Trying to get an idea of the size of these tracks, each of the boys placed a foot in one of the tracks. Looking at each other, they were surprised: even with two feet in the print, they still were not able to cover it. Crouching down and looking closely, they estimated the print was about sixteen inches long and about eight inches wide. They had found proof of the skunk ape! They raced back to the house to tell Marilena.

That afternoon, Joe called home to see how everything was going. That's when my sister told him about the tracks the boys had found in the back. Joe told my sister not to let the boys wander too far off until he had a chance to investigate. In the meantime, Al and Anthony went out to play with the other kids, and they told them about the footprints. The kids told the boys that the sheriff had added more patrols because of the increase in sightings of the creature. It seemed that this summer, more than any before, was turning out to be an extremely active one for the skunk ape.

Joe came home on his break. The boys excitedly brought him to the spot where they saw the footprints. When they got there, they saw tracks from dirt bikes instead. It seemed that a few of the older kids in the area decided to have a race through the swamp, and in doing so, they destroyed the tracks made by the creature. Al and Anthony were devastated; they had hoped to make plaster-of-paris casts of the footprints for souvenirs. Frustrated, Joe and the boys headed back to the coolness of the air-conditioned house.

For about a week nothing more was heard (or smelled) from their friend the skunk ape. Then, one morning, while my sister was shopping, she ran into a friend whose farm was just down the road from their house.

Being neighborly, my sister asked, "Hi, Marjorie. So what's new with you and Hank (her husband)?"

This is what Marjorie recounted to my sister: "Well, the night before last, Hank and I had the fright of their lives. That evening, we were about to sit down to dinner when we heard the horses in the corral making a racket. My husband got up from the table and looked out the window to see what the problem was. To his astonishment, he saw a huge creature chasing the horses around the corral. He got his shotgun, opened the door, and set the dogs on the creature; then he started for the corral.

"The creature, hearing the dogs barking and seeing my husband coming, started running for the fence. My husband raised his shotgun and shot. He missed the creature, but he did manage to put a sizable hole in the barn. The creature looked back at him, and with one giant leap, it cleared the fence and headed back into the woods. My husband called the sheriff and reported the incident.

"When the sheriff and the deputies arrived, my husband brought them to the corral to show them what the creature had done to the horse. My husband called the horse over. The horse, still spooked, walked gingerly toward them and stopped. Then my husband pointed to the hindquarters of the horse. There, as plain as day, were ten finger marks scarred into the horse. One of the deputies remarked about how big the hands had to have been and the strength they needed to have in order to leave those marks. The hands must have been huge.

"Then my husband showed them where he had last seen the creature entering the woods, but after an hour of searching, they were not able to find anything. However, before leaving, the sheriff promised to step up the patrols in the area."

Shocked, Marilena replied, "Not too long ago, my brother and cousin heard something strange in our backyard. I guess there must be some truth about the skunk ape being back."

My sister and her friend ended their conversation with the usual promise to keep in touch.

Upon returning home, Marilena told the boys about the encounter Marjorie and Hank had had the other night. Both Al and Anthony gave each other a look, "Oh, oh! This thing is for real, and it is hanging around here!"

A Second Encounter with the Skunk Ape

As fate would have it, my sister and Joe were planning to take some friends who were visiting from New York to Miami for a day of shopping and sightseeing. They told Al and Anthony if they ran into any problems to call the sheriff and to not try to handle things themselves. Being left with that reassuring thought, Al, Anthony, and the kids settled down for an afternoon of swimming and a night of sandwiches and ice cream.

It was close to 9:00 p.m. when the boys put the kids to bed. Afterward, Al and Anthony, each brandishing a bowl of popcorn, sat down to watch TV. Not even an hour had gone by when they heard a strange howl.

At the sound, my sister's dog, Grizzly, sprang to his feet and started to bark relentlessly. As Al and Anthony worked to calm Grizzly, they got a whiff of that same nasty odor, which this time seemed much stronger. Then, in an instant, all of the house's outside security lights went on. Al and Anthony were facing the front picture window and saw a large silhouette projected on the drawn shade, slowly crossing from left to right.

The silhouette had to be at least eight feet tall and the shoulders were probably five feet wide. The figure was massive!

The boys ran into the kitchen and looked for something they could use to protect themselves. Al picked up a hammer, and Anthony grabbed a butcher knife. With Grizzly barking at their side, the boys were ready to do what they had to protect themselves and the kids who were sleeping in their rooms.

Just as quickly as the episode started, it ended. Everything became quiet; it was an eerie stillness. Grizzly had stopped barking, so Anthony found enough courage to peek out the window to see if the creature was still there. Looking across the yard, he thought he saw someone or something bending down and taking a drink from the pond on the next property. Whatever it was quickly jumped up and ran into the woods.

As if to verify that everything had returned to normal, the security lights all turned off. Grizzly was just panting and looking to go outside to do his thing. Breathing easier, the boys checked on the kids. To their surprise, they were fast asleep. The boys went back into the family room and nervously waited for Joe and Marilena to come home.

It was about 11:00 p.m. when my sister and her husband returned home. As soon as they opened the door the boys rushed up and told them what had occurred.

Joe asked, "Why didn't you call the sheriff?"

The boys just looked at each other, dumbfounded, and said, "I don't know. I guess we were so scared that we didn't even think of it!"

Joe asked, "Did you see which way it headed?"

Anthony said, "I think I saw it go around the pond and into the woods—toward the horse farm."

Joe told the boys "Go put on your shoes and get in the car. I want to see this thing for myself."

While the boys were putting on their shoes, Joe went to his room and from the top shelf of the closet grabbed his 45-caliber pistol. Joe was dead set on getting this mystery solved.

Tracking the Skunk Ape

As they left the driveway, Joe made a left and slowly headed toward the horse farm. Meanwhile, Al and Anthony shined their flashlights along the shoulders of the road. Al directed his light on the right shoulder, and Anthony shined his on the left side of the road. As they approached the one-lane bridge on their right, Joe spotted two sheriff's cars coming over the bridge. Once over the bridge, the one car went left, passing by Joe, and the other went to the right. Joe decided he would follow the one with the sheriff in it, since he probably knew his way around better than the deputy did.

The road they were on formed a square. Joe guessed that the sheriff was going one way and the deputy was going the other way to see if they could corner whatever they were trying to catch. Joe continued to follow the sheriff, going slowly and staying a reasonable distance behind.

About five minutes had passed when Joe saw the headlights from the deputy's car coming toward them from the west. Everything was very quiet and still. The sheriff slowly crept down the road, aiming his spotlight into the woods. Joe, still behind him, crawled along too, listening and looking all around. Suddenly, they heard a large crash. Looking ahead, they saw what looked like smoke coming from the deputy's car engine; and its right headlight was burnt out. The sheriff sped up to the deputy, who was standing outside the vehicle.

Joe made his way to the two officers, pulled his car over, and then he and the boys proceeded to the deputy's car. To their surprise, the deputy's car was a total wreck!

Joe asked the officers, "Is everyone okay?"

The sheriff answered, "He is, but I don't think that the car is."

The deputy started to explain just what happened. "As I was coming down the road, I was scanning the right side of the woods. Out of nowhere, this huge thing came running from my left and crossed right in front of my car. I was probably going about fifteen miles per hour when I hit the thing."

The sheriff, scratching his head, said, "Are you sure you didn't hit a tree?"

The deputy answered, "A tree? Here in the middle of the road?" The deputy continued, "Look over here." He pointed to the street sign that was almost bent in half and said, "This is where it landed when I hit it. Then the thing got up, turned, and screamed at me before it took off into the woods."

The sheriff, trying to calm down his deputy and break the obvious tension, jokingly said, "Why didn't you chase the thing down? You have a shotgun and a dog, don't you?"

Everyone smiled but the deputy.

The deputy replied, "Hell, I wouldn't go in there with an AK-47 and fifty dogs. Besides, I was waiting for some brave law officer like you to come by and lead the way."

His comeback got a big laugh from everyone. The sheriff called in the accident. He asked for a wrecker and for assistance from the state police.

A few minutes later, a few more deputies arrived with tracking dogs. The little country road was starting to get crowded. Joe and the boys stayed out of the way and just listened to what the authorities planned to do. They noticed a farmer, who had arrived just after the accident occurred, talking to one of the deputies.

Joe overheard the farmer say, "Well, all this started over on my farm earlier tonight."

Joe, being inquisitive, went over and asked the farmer, "Does this have to do with the skunk ape? If it does, you should know that the thing was over at my house earlier this evening too."

The farmer said, "It sure does! That SOB killed one of my prize bulls!"

Joe asked, "How did he manage that?"

The farmer replied, "The thing must have been crossing the pasture when the bull spotted him. That bull does not like anyone coming close to his territory."

My brother Al could vouch for that; there were a number of times that he had used the pasture as a shortcut to my sister's house and the bull had chased him.

The farmer continued, "I figured the bull must have gone after the creature. However, this thing did not run away. It must have stood its ground and killed the damn bull."

Joe asked, "How can you kill a two-ton bull?"

The farmer answered, "If you're that creature, you pull the bull's head right off its shoulders!"

Joe was shocked, "That's incredible!"

The farmer said, "Drive about two miles down this road, and you'll see some yellow construction tape on the barbwire. I put it up to mark the spot for the sheriff. Look about eight feet to left of the tape, and you will see the torso. And about fifteen feet to the left of the torso, you'll see the bull's head."

Checking Out the Evidence

Joe and the boys stood there, stunned by what the farmer had told them. Just then, the state police helicopter was heard overhead. The sheriff and a state police captain were organizing a search party for the creature. The sheriff came over to Joe and said that he and the boys should go home and keep an eye out for the creature there.

Joe and the boys got back into the car and headed home, but they had to make one stop. They wanted to see the dead bull for themselves. They went a couple of miles down the road and saw the yellow tape just as the farmer had described. Nervously, they got out of the car with their flashlights in hand and marked off the number steps to where they expected to see the torso.

There it was. At first it was hard to distinguish the beast in the dark. However, once all the flashlights concentrated on the area, there could be no mistake. There was the bull's torso, covered with insects; all four legs were pointing skyward. They slowly started walking to where they believed they would find the bull's head. Scanning the ground with their flashlights, they finally came across the horrific site. With the flashlights pointing directly on the bull's head, they could see its horns, its tongue hanging out, and its wide-open eyes. After gawking at the gruesome remains for what seemed to my brother a lifetime, Joe and the boys hurried back to car and headed for home.

My brother told me that after this incident, things started to calm down. The skunk ape sightings became less frequent during the rest of the summer. There were a couple of nights when they thought they might have heard something strange, but with the woods and swamp so close, it could have been anything. As for the odor, my brother told me that that, too, seemed to be occurring less.

Two years later, Marilena and her family moved from Davies to Daytona. Both Al and Anthony were getting older and starting to spend their summers back in Yonkers, hanging out with their friends. However, my sister tells me that even now, reports continue about people seeing the skunk ape.

The Connecticut UFO Encounter

This next narrative is about Al's introduction to the UFO phenomena. But before chronicling this account, let me provide a little background on what Al thought of my association with paranormal investigations and research, especially where it concerned UFOs.

Every time I told Al about a sighting I had investigated or was researching, he would guffaw and ask, "How can you believe that stuff? People who tell you they see strange things in the sky either do not know what they are looking at or are crazy. My opinion is I think most of them are crazy."

That was my brother's opinion regarding UFOs before the night of July 24, 1984. Here is the incident that not only changed his mind but also his life.

It's Going up Main Street!

It was the evening of July 24, 1984. I had finished dinner and was painting one of the rooms in my brother Al's apartment, which was on the third floor of our home in Bridgeport, Connecticut. Often, when I would paint, I would listen to a talk show called *The Tiny Markel Show*. But on that night, the usual subject matter changed quickly. A caller to the show excitedly announced to Tiny and the audience that there was a giant UFO slowly heading up Main Street.

Tiny joked, "I wish that thing better luck trying to find a parking space than I had today."

The caller, getting agitated, told Tiny, "Look out your damn window if you don't believe me."

Tiny excused himself and told the audience he would be right back while he satisfied the caller's request. Well, needless to say, this caught my interest. I stopped painting and waited anxiously for Tiny's report. After what seemed like forever, but was really only about a minute, Tiny came back on the air.

"Folks," Tiny eagerly exclaimed, "the caller is not joking. I can see what looks like a huge craft, about a couple of hundred feet above the buildings downtown, going up Main Street!" Tiny continued, "I'm going to run up to the roof to see if I can get a better look at this thing. I'll be back in a couple."

After his announcement, the radio started playing commercials.

I started talking to myself, "If this thing is heading up Main Street, it's coming my way!"

Racing through the Streets of Bridgeport

I dropped my paintbrush, ran into my room, grabbed my binoculars and camera, and raced out the door. I rushed to the car and turned on the radio to hear any new developments on the UFO.

I placed myself in the middle of the street and looked east toward Main Street, which was only a block away. I couldn't see a thing. I thought to myself, *What happened to the damn thing?* According to the last report, the object was headed north on Main Street. It would have to pass right where I could see it, but there was nothing there. I went back to the car, got in and turned on the radio to hear the latest on what was happening.

Tiny was back on the radio and said that from what he could tell, the object had changed its course and was now heading northwest toward Park Avenue. That meant it was heading toward Sacred Heart University. I decided to head it off by going up Madison Avenue and then cutting over toward Park Avenue. I should have no problem beating it there. I started the car and raced toward Madison Avenue.

Talk about bad luck. I no sooner got to Madison Avenue than I had to stop because of police cars racing up the road. Once they passed, I took off, but it was to no avail. I caught a red light at the next corner. Let me tell you, if there weren't three cars in front of me, I would have gone through the light.

Finally, I arrived on Park Avenue; the tree line was a lot lower there, and so I was able to see more of the sky. I searched the sky while driving toward Sacred Heart University. Then I heard on the radio that a caller had said that the UFO was being observed over the town of Fairfield and was heading north toward the Merritt Parkway. At this point, I gave up the chase. From where I was to where the UFO was last seen was about five miles, and there was no way I was going to be able to catch up with it. I turned the car around and headed back for home.

As I came into the house, my wife Lois asked, "Where did you go? I went upstairs thinking you were painting, but I saw the paint brush in the tray, and you were nowhere to be found."

I explained what had happened and that I had thought I would finally get a good look at a UFO and capture it on film. She just shook her head and went back to getting the kids ready for bed. I went upstairs to finish my painting.

A Close Encounter of a Third Kind

It was about 9:15 p.m., when the front door burst open, and I heard Al call out for me. I called back, telling him I was upstairs in his apartment, painting. I heard him racing up the stairs.

He rushed in, pale and wide-eyed, and said, "You'll never guess what I saw!"

I answered him, self-satisfied, knowing exactly what he saw. "You saw a UFO, right?"

Al stood there, shocked, and asked, "How the hell did you know that?"

I told him about the radio broadcast and my escapade through the streets of Bridgeport's north end.

He asked, "So you saw it, too?"

I answered, "No, I never got close enough even to see it from a distance. How about you, did you get a good view of it?"

Al came back with, "Did I ever! Let me tell you about it."

What follows is my brother's account of what happened on the night of July 24, 1984.

Al was on his way home, traveling northbound on the Merritt Parkway. He had just passed exit 42 in Westport, and noticing that it was almost 8:00 p.m., he decided to switch the radio to the Yankee game. Al settled in to listen to the game, but just a couple of minutes later he noticed that the radio was picking up a lot of static. He fumbled with the dial, but it kept getting worse. As he began climbing the hill toward exit 44 in Fairfield, his car started sputtering as if it was getting ready to stall. When he reached the top of the hill, the sputtering got worse. Not wanting to stop on the highway, Al guided the car off the road, where it finally stalled out.

Al got out of the car to investigate what might have caused his engine to stall. As he started walking to the front of his car, he noticed that down the hill from him, the traffic was stopped dead on both sides of the highway, right at the exit ramps. Al figured that no one would be going anywhere with that backup and decided to go down the hill and see what the problem was. He saw a state trooper standing in the center divider and walked over to him to find out what was going on.

Al reached the trooper and asked, "What happened?"

The trooper answered, "Look up."

He looked up and could not believe his eyes. About 150 feet above them was an object that covered the entire four lanes and both shoulders of the highway. It was so huge that it even stretched over the Fairfield Inn, which was about 200 feet off the exit. From what Al could determine, the object had to be at least 300 to 400 feet wide. To Al, it looked as if someone had taken Giant Stadium and placed it in the air. It was not only unbelievably wide, but if it were on the ground, it would have been as tall as a six-story building.

Still amazed, Al noticed that under the craft there were hundreds of lights; it looked like a small city upside down in the sky. All this time the trooper was trying to communicate with the dispatcher on his walkie-talkie, but he was getting nothing.

At this point in the story, I asked Al if he had seen the object as he was walking down the hill, but he said he was busy looking around to see if there were any cars wrecked in the bushes, and he hadn't looked up. I also asked if there were other people looking at the object. He said there were about one hundred people standing around on the northbound side where the trooper and he were talking, and probably fifty or sixty people were on the southbound side. There were also a lot of people who were afraid to get out of their cars.

Al and the trooper were still standing in the center divide. Al asked, "What do you think that is?"

The trooper frustrated that his walkie-talkie was not working, answered abruptly, "What does it look like? It's a UFO!"

As huge as it was, it made no sound. The whole vicinity was blanketed with an eerie silence. The craft hovered only one hundred feet or so above the trees but did not trigger even one leaf to budge.

After watching the craft for about ten minutes, Al saw it suddenly climb from one hundred feet to about one thousand feet in a blink of an eye. As soon as that happened, all of the cars began to start up on their own, and the trooper's walkie-talkie became active.

Once the trooper's radio started working, he called the dispatcher. The trooper said in a commanding voice, "Notify the air national guard, and have them send a couple of jets here, between exits 44 and 46 on the Merritt Parkway, ASAP. We have a UFO sitting right on top of us."

With their car engines running again, some people left, but most remained to watch, hoping to see what the huge UFO was going to do next.

The Air Force Arrives

It had only been about twenty minutes since Al arrived on the hill when the UFO shot up into the night sky and disappeared.

No more than thirty seconds after the trooper had called for the jets, an enormous roar came from the east just above the trees. Two F14 jets shot by, no more than two hundred feet above the scene.

People rushed to get into their cars to get away from the deafening noise. Al, still standing next to the trooper, heard the voice of one of the pilots coming over the trooper's radio.

The pilot asked, "Where is this thing? We haven't seen anything on our radar since leaving the base."

The trooper answered, "You just missed it. It shot up and out of sight just a couple of seconds before you got here."

The pilot replied, "We'll check out the area."

Al could see the jets make sweeping turns, scouring the area. After a second flyby, the pilots got back on the radio to notify the trooper that they did not see anything visually or on their radar and were heading back to their base.

The people who remained seemed to be walking around in a stupor. Al could hear them questioning each other about what they had just witnessed, trying to make sense of it.

The trooper shouted out to the remaining crowd, "Does anyone want to make out a report about this?" No one answered; everyone just got in their cars and took off.

I looked at my brother and asked, "Well, are you now a believer?"

Al said, "I'll never joke about flying saucers again!"

My brother has kept his word about this. Well, he really has had no choice. As you will see, this was only the beginning of Al's encounters.

However, before we leave this account, I would like to add a few comments of my own. I did a little investigating on this sighting. When digging deeper into the mystery, there were a few questions that I never received satisfactory answers for:

- The following morning on the radio, a number of callers said they had notified Bridgeport Airport about the UFO but were told that the airport had no information regarding this incident. If hundreds of people on the ground saw this huge object, why couldn't the radar people at our local airport see it?

- And how did the jets get there so fast? Did they already know that there was an unknown object in the area before the trooper's call?

- That same night, there were numerous reports coming from the Hudson River valley (New York) area, which is about twenty miles from Fairfield, Connecticut. Nevertheless, for some unknown reason, they were never mentioned in conjunction with Al's incident in any of the New York or Connecticut newspapers.

Well, I don't want to beat a dead horse here. For whatever reason, hundreds of people in Fairfield County know what transpired that evening. As my brother said, "Just on the parkway alone, over a hundred of us saw this huge thing. How can the people at the airport say they did not see it on radar or claim they did not get any calls about it? I just don't understand."

I guess we'll never understand the cover-up and denial from our authorities.

Twinkle, Twinkle Little Star?

Al's next encounter took place during the last week of January 1994. He and his friend Lenny experienced what is known as a "close encounter of the second kind."

It was 6:00 p.m., and Al and Lenny had just signed out from their post office jobs at the north Yonkers (New York) station. As the two started for the back parking lot, they engaged in small talk about the day's events. Stepping off the loading dock, they commented that although the night seemed abnormally dark and brutally cold, at least it was clear, and they did not have to worry about driving home in a snowstorm. They were walking briskly toward their cars when Al spotted what he believed to be an unusually bright star in the night sky.

He pointed out the star to Lenny and said, "Don't you think that star is blinking kind of strange? The others aren't as intense as that one."

Lenny stared at the star and commented back with conviction, "No, when it's as cold as it is tonight, the stars seem brighter. It's something to do with the cold and the atmosphere."

As they got to their cars, Al glanced up and thought that something was very strange about that star. He called over to Lenny and said, "Hey, Lenny, watch this."

Al got into his car and turned his lights on and off several times. All of a sudden, the "star" started gliding toward them. From what Al could estimate, when he and Lenny first saw it, it was probably about a mile away. It was now only a couple of hundred yards away and had stopped just above a line of trees that were located in the empty field in front of them.

Lenny, visibly nervous, told Al not to mess around with it anymore. Al could not believe what had just happened; he turned his lights on and off three more times. To Al and Lenny's surprise, the "star" responded by flashing three times and emitting three small, red spheres from its underbelly. The spheres were dropped about five seconds apart. As each reached about thirty feet from the ground, the sphere turned off, as if you were turning off an electric light with a switch. When Al and Lenny looked upward after watching the spheres drop, the "star" was no longer there.

Hell, That's No Stealth Aircraft!

Scanning the sky to see where the "star" might have gone, they looked to the left and then to the right, but it was nowhere to be found. Then Al got an uneasy compulsion to look straight up. There it was! But what they thought was a "star" was a triangular object, hovering no more than one hundred feet above them.

The object took on a blackish-gray appearance in the night sky. They could see what looked like giant spotlights on each of the corners, but they were not on. From what Al could determine, the object was about 300 feet in length (sides) and about 150 feet wide (base/back). They watched as the object turned 120 degrees by keeping the front point stationary and swinging the rest of the craft's body to the left. It was as if the object was on an axis and pivoting. Once it completed its turn, it slowly started to drift to the west.

Lenny excitedly exclaimed, "That must be some new stealth aircraft the military has!"

Al answered, "Hell, that's no stealth aircraft; if it was a stealth aircraft, we would have heard the engines roaring. Plus, they don't just float. As slow as that thing is going, any normal aircraft would have crashed."

The guys watched for just a minute longer and decided it was time to head for home and get away from the strange object. Al and Lenny jumped into their cars and drove off in opposite directions. Just for peace of mind, when Al got home he went up to the roof of his apartment to make sure that the object had not followed him. Can't say that I blame him.

I don't know, but it does seem strange that my brother has had all these encounters, and someone like me, who has been doing this for years, has never seen anything I could call a UFO.

Are You Following Me?

Continuing with my brother's UFO encounters, the next incident occurred on the night of January 16, 2004. My brother and his daughter Amanda were readying to return home after "Family Night" at Amanda's marital arts school. The school was located in Hopewell Junction, New York, which was about ten miles from their home in LaGrange, New York. During "Family Night," Al and the other parents participated in the class exercises with the kids. Amanda, ten years old, enjoyed being with the other kids. And learning how to protect herself increased her self-confidence.

Hey, Dad, I Think There's a UFO Following Us

It was another one of those extremely cold January nights, when every bone in your body is begging for that proverbial "January thaw" to show up. Running to the car, Al and Amanda got in for the thirty-minute ride from Hopewell Junction back home to LaGrange.

Al started the engine and turned on the heater. Waiting while the car warmed up, he asked Amanda, "Did you have a good time?"

Amanda happily answered, "Yes, Dad, and I wish every Friday night was "Family Night" so you could work out with us."

With the car warmed up, they started for home. They had been traveling for about ten minutes and were just at the junction of route 376 and route 21, when Amanda, who was buckled in the backseat, called to her father, "Hey, Dad, I think there's a UFO following us."

Al asked, "What? Where?"

Amanda answered, "To your left; look out the window."

Al quickly glanced to the left and behind him he saw what he believed was an airplane. He answered Amanda, "That's just an airplane; the Dutchess County Airport is only about two miles from here."

Amanda said, "I don't think so. It's been following us for a while."

Al decided to pull the car over to see if the "airplane" would go by so that they could get better look. When he stopped, the "airplane" stopped too, about two hundred yards from them.

Amanda said, "You see, I told you it was a UFO; airplanes can't stop like that."

Al responded, "Well, maybe it's a helicopter. We'll see what happens when we get closer to the airport."

As they reached the road that led to the airport, they noticed that whatever had been following them had turned south, toward Wappingers Falls and the airport. Al, convinced it was just an aircraft, continued toward home. Meanwhile, Amanda, not convinced it was an airplane, continued to search the dark January night sky.

Come out Quick, There's a UFO Right over Our House!

Reaching home, both Amanda and Al prepared to dash through the below-freezing cold to their warm house. Just as Al was closing the car door, he had this strange urge to look up. To his surprise, the same type of object he and his friend Lenny had seen ten years ago was back and perched only one hundred feet over his house! The object was so huge that it sprawled over both of their neighbor's houses with Al's house being in the center.

Amanda saw her dad looking up, and she looked up too. Stunned at what she saw, she ran into the house to get her mother.

Amanda's mother, Kathy, watched her daughter run into the house and almost fall on her face. Kathy shouted, "Slow down! What's wrong?"

Amanda answered excitedly, "Come out, quick; there's a UFO right over our house!"

Kathy dropped what she was doing and ran out to see what was going on. She saw Al, very absorbed, looking at the object suspended over their house.

She breathlessly asked Al, "What is that?"

Al responded, "It's a UFO, and it looks exactly like what Lenny and I saw ten years ago in Yonkers!" He then told Kathy, "Go in the house and get me the Maglite flashlight, my samurai sword, and the dog."

Kathy rushed into the house to get Al what he asked for. Meanwhile, Al watched the jet-black object silently and slowly drifts north toward the woods and power lines across the street and then stop.

By this time Kathy had come out with the light, the sword, and the dog.

Al said to Kathy, "Look, if I don't come back within a half an hour, call the police, and tell them where I was headed."

With that, Al headed toward the woods where the object was hovering.

The Object Just Vanished

As Al walked up the street about one hundred or so yards away from the object, he noticed it drop three red globes—just as he had witnessed ten years ago. Intent on finding what the globes could be, he quickened his pace toward the object. At about seventy-five yards away, as the red globes were halfway from the ground, they suddenly switched off, as if someone had turned off a light.

Wanting to know what this thing was dropping, Al started running to the spot where he thought the globes would have hit the ground.

About thirty yards from where he thought the globes would be Al flashed his Maglite three times. To his surprise, the object returned the gesture and flashed a strobe three times. With that, the object just vanished. Although stunned at what he had witnessed, Al continued to the area where he believed the globes had hit the ground.

For the next ten minutes, Al thoroughly examined the area where he saw the globes fall, but he was not able to find anything except leaves and twigs littering the ground. He checked the air for any kind of odor that the globes or the strange object might have left behind, but he could not smell anything. He finally gave up the search and started back to the house.

Reflecting on what he just witnessed, a few things still troubled Al. First was, how did the object know where he lived? Second, he wondered if it was the same object that Lenny and he had seen back in 1994. From all characteristics, it gave the impression it was. And finally, he wondered why the dog, which was in the middle of the entire goings on, didn't bark once or show any kind of interest.

As Al headed back to the house, he could see Kathy on the deck with her cell phone in her hand.

Kathy said, "I was just about to call the police. You were gone for almost an hour, and I was getting worried. Then, thank God, I saw the light from your flashlight, and I figured you were okay. Did you find anything?"

Al answered, "No, not a thing. Come on, let's go in. I'm freezing."

In recounting his experiences to me, my brother was baffled as to why he has had so many of these encounters. I suggested that if this should happen again, he should seek a reputable hypnotist. The hypnotist might be able to take him hypnotically back (regressive hypnosis) to these incidents and see if there are reasons for him having these experiences. Until then, we will just have to wait to see what happens to Al next.

Aunt Valeria and the "Gaetano Trilogy"

The next three accounts were given to me by Aunt Valeria regarding some strange occurrences surrounding my Aunt Adriana's husband Gaetano ("Guy" in English) Nicolari's death. I call them the "Gaetano Trilogy."

The Restless Spirit

The first incident occurred in June 1942. Aunt Adriana's husband, Gaetano, had been suffering from ALS (amyotrophic lateral sclerosis, commonly called Lou Gehrig's disease) for a while. Sensing he had, at best, only a few months to live, Uncle Gaetano decided to rent a bungalow in the Catskill Mountains of upstate New York where he could enjoy the company of his lovely family: Aunt Adriana and their two infant children—Roland, two and a half, and Yvonne, ten months. He rented a cabin in Catskill, New York, only a couple of hours from their home in Yonkers.

The family spent three great days together and were packing for their return home. Having had a busy day of swimming and picnicking, they decided to retire early that evening so that they could get an early start back to the city in the morning. After only a few hours of sleep, for some unknown reason, Aunt Adriana was jolted awake.

Looking toward the kitchen area, she noticed what seemed to be a figure of a man pacing back and forth in a worried state. She suddenly realized the man was Gaetano.

She shouted to him, "Gaetano, what are you doing? Come back to bed."

The figure, as though it heard her, turned toward my aunt and slowly faded away. Aunt Adriana, sitting up in bed, could not believe what she had just witnessed. Turning her head and looking down to her side, she saw Gaetano quietly sleeping. Stunned by the event, my aunt understandably was not able to get back to sleep. The following morning, she promised herself not to mention her experience to Gaetano; he had enough to be concerned with and did not need this on top of everything else.

Once back home, my aunt told both my grandmother (her mother) and Aunt Valeria (her sister) about the strange thing that had occurred.

My grandmother, being the quintessential old-country oracle, soothsayer, and mystic, said, "This is a sign of a troubled spirit; knowing he won't be long for this world, he worries for the family he will leave behind."

Aunt Adriana asked, "What can we do to help?"

My grandmother answered, "We need to pray for his soul and pray that his spirit finds peace with its destiny."

Raised by my grandmother and knowing her all too well, her answer did not surprise me. She was always both the voice of prayers and the voice of doom. Even though she is gone now, I still love and miss my Nonna dearly.

The Visitor

Aunt Valeria described the second eerie event having to do with the passing of my Uncle Gaetano. This one occurred on the day before my uncle's passing, on August 28, 1942.

No prayers in the world could stop the swift decline of Uncle Gaetano's health. It was evident that he was nearing the end of his relatively short life. Every day, concerned neighbors and friends would stop by to see if they could be of any help to Aunt Adriana and her family. One such neighbor was Florence, who, with her husband Bill, lived in the apartment next door. Florence and Bill not only were my aunt's friends but also were very close with the rest of our family. In fact, they were considered part of our extended family.

Elderly Man Coming up the Stairs

As I mentioned, Florence and Bill were next-door neighbors and very good friends of the family. On this day, Florence was getting ready to do some shopping and had gone next door to ask my aunt if she needed anything. Those were the good old days when you could leave your door open for your neighbors and friends. My aunt said she did not need anything and thanked her for asking.

Florence slowly started down the back stairs, and when she was about halfway down, she unexpectedly ran into an elderly man coming up. The man, who was sporting an overgrown mustache and a large black hat, seemed to be the kind of person you would associate as a peasant farmer. Speaking to Florence in Italian, he stated he was on his way to visit the children. Thinking nothing of it, Florence smiled and continued down the stairs.

Later that evening, Florence stopped by my aunt's as she often did to see if she needed any help before turning in for the night. During their casual conversation, Florence asked my aunt about the man who had visited her that afternoon. Florence, knowing my aunt's acquaintances, had not recognized this person and wondered if he was someone from out of town.

My aunt, acting puzzled, asked Florence whom she was talking about, because she hadn't had any visitors all afternoon.

Florence answered, "The elderly Italian gentleman, the one with the mustache and large black hat."

My aunt, still puzzled, replied, "No, no one was here. I don't know who you could be asking about."

Florence, clearly confused, said, "I remember him saying he was on his way to see the children, and since you're the only other apartment on this floor, I assumed he was speaking about your children, Yvonne and Roland."

Both bewildered, they shrugged their shoulders, said good night, and parted for the evening. Later that same night, Uncle Gaetano finally succumbed to his fatal disease.

Man in the Photograph

About a week after my uncle's burial, my aunt was putting away some old photographs when Florence stopped by with freshly baked cookies. Placing the dish of cookies on the table, Florence noticed a familiar face in one of the photographs. Looking closer, she recognized the man in the photograph as the same man who had passed her on the stairs a week ago.

Florence excitingly pointed to the man in the photograph and said, "This is the man I ran into on the stairs last week."

Very puzzled, my aunt shook her head and said, "No, this can't be him; this is Gaetano's father. His father lives in Naples and has never been to America."

Years after that incident, Florence continued to stick to her story. She insisted that the man she had seen on the stairs was the same man in the photograph.

Could this have been what is known in the paranormal world as *astral projection*—the act of separating the astral body (spirit or consciousness) from the physical body so that it can journey into the universal plane? Could astral projection be due to a father's wish to be with his son and his family at this time of great emotional stress? Remember, Florence's encounter occurred just an hour before Gaetano's passing.

I asked Aunt Valeria if they ever tried to get in touch with Gaetano's father to see if they could confirm Florence's experience, but she could not recall if anything further came of it. Our family just passed it off as one of those mysterious acts of God.

The Specter

The third and final installment in the "Gaetano Trilogy" occurred shortly after Uncle Gaetano's passing. My grandfather found a bigger apartment, not only for his family (my grandmother, Aunt Valeria, and my father), but also for Aunt Adriana and her two children. The apartment was located on Highland Avenue in Yonkers, which was not far from their old one, enabling them to stay in close contact with rest of the family and their friends.

A number of months had passed, and Aunt Valeria felt that things were getting somewhat back to normal—that is, until the evening of November 1, 1942, All Saints Day.

It started just like any other evening, with my aunts putting Roland and Yvonne to bed and then getting themselves ready for a night of long-awaited rest.

The bedroom, which my aunts shared, happened to be located at the rear of the house and was the last room before entering the enclosed back porch. Being the last room in the apartment and butting up against the porch, the bedroom lacked good lighting; it was dreadful, to say the least. This always frustrated my aunts when they tried to do anything in there. The two small windows looking out to the porch did not help to relieve the dark situation.

As they were pulling the bedcovers down, my aunts' attention was drawn toward the porch windows. They stared intently as a shadowy form started to take shape. Slowly the form developed into a silhouette of a person lying in a casket. Unmistakably the silhouette was of Gaetano.

Both of my aunts looked in astonishment as the silhouette started to fade and finally dissipated into thin air.

Trying to make sense of what had just happened, my aunts went out on the porch, thinking that someone walking around with a flashlight or a candle could have caused it. However, once on the porch, they noticed nothing usual or out of place. Not knowing what could have caused the vision, they quietly returned to their room to get some much-needed sleep; they were still mystified and never mentioned the incident again.

Could this have been a figment of their imaginations or some kind of suggestive hallucination (where the power of invention of one person influences others into believing something that does not exist)? Could the fact that it was All Saints Day have influenced my aunts' psyches?

According to Aunt Valeria, All Saints Day did not have any bearing on what they saw. She made it clear that it had been almost three months since Gaetano was buried. Although there was always talk about a "presence" of Gaetano around the house, why all of a sudden would they have this vision on that particular night? My aunt did not buy any of the suggestions I put forth; she said insistently, "We saw it and that's that!"

Cousin Claudia's
Spooky Summer Home in Italy

The following accounts revolve around my cousin Claudia, her family, and her home in Tagliacozzo, Italy.

I would like to make it perfectly clear that I know my cousin's character and integrity to be of the highest stratum. This gives credence to these reports and explains why they cannot be dismissed or ignored.

Haunting Footsteps

My cousin's first paranormal experience occurred in 1971 at the age sixteen while visiting the family summer home in Tagliacozzo, Italy.

Claudia, her mother, and her father were enjoying another typical, lovely, summer afternoon in beautiful Tagliacozzo. Like most afternoons, her parents were looking forward to driving into town and stopping at the *piazza* (town square) for coffee. However, today Claudia did not want to go. She wanted to stay home and be alone.

Getting permission from her parents, she was thrilled—for the next several hours she would have the whole house to herself. She stood, peeking out the window, watching her mother and father getting into the car. Claudia paid special attention to the automatic security gate to be certain that it closed and locked firmly behind them as they drove off. At that time, their house was the only home for miles. They were isolated, and there was nothing around them except an old cemetery about a quarter mile down the road.

Who's There?

Knowing that all the doors and windows were locked, Claudia started upstairs to get her records. Suddenly, from below, she heard the door to the kitchen open and then close. She stood very still, and she heard the sound of footsteps walking into the kitchen and continuing into the living room.

Claudia thought to herself, *who could that be? How did someone get into the house without anyone knowing?* At the time of this incident, the home was only five years old. Therefore, we can eliminate the creaky old house and house-settling syndromes. The other thing to note is that most homes in Italy have marble floors, which tend to echo loudly, and there is no mistaking when you hear footsteps.

There Claudia stood, in the upstairs hallway, frozen in place. She knew there was no one else in the house or anywhere outside, but she had distinctly heard footsteps.

She waited for a moment, and then called out, "Who's there?"

There was no answer. At this point, she became terrified. From where she stood, she was able to see below into the living room. Scanning the living room, Claudia could see no one. Then, calling on every ounce of her being, she ran into the bathroom and locked herself in. Still scared out of her wits, she quietly walked over to the bathroom window and watched the front door below for three hours, during which time nothing or no one ever came out of the home. Those were the longest three hours of her life!

Something Walked in and Never Left That House

Claudia finally saw her parents' car approach the gate and continue up the driveway. She frantically ran out to tell them what had happened. To her disappointment, her parents laughed it off as if she were crazy and told her that it was just her imagination running wild. Even to this day, when Claudia mentions the event of that afternoon, people do not believe her and smirk about it. However, she is firmly convinced that something walked into that house and never left.

If you should question Claudia about this, she will adamantly tell you, "I know it was real; it did happen, and I will never forget it."

The Analysis

Looking further into this incident, I asked Claudia about the surroundings. Specifically, I asked about the age of the road in front of the house and if she had any idea when the road was built.

She answered, "The road was built by the Romans over two thousand years ago and was part of the Appian Way, a network of ancient roads. At that time, Tagliacozzo was a Roman outpost located in the Apennine Mountains."

Having this information, I proposed to Claudia, "Do you think that a lost soul who once traveled the road now wanders it aimlessly?"

There were other possibilities too. Claudia and her grandfather had had a caring relationship; it could have been that her grandfather, while taking an afternoon nap, had an out-of-body experience (OBE). This is where a person's spiritual body leaves the physical body during an unusually deep sleep.

And let us not forget about the old cemetery down the road. There are hundreds of accounts of people living near cemeteries who have witnessed apparitions and ghostly figures in their homes. Maybe some poor souls did not realize their time here was up and they needed to move on.

Those are some of theories I proposed to Claudia.

She responded, "Take your pick; it could be any of them."

Don't Worry, the Spirit of Grandfather Is Watching You

The second event involving the home in Tagliacozzo occurred to Claudia's cousin Nicolina. Nicolina recounted the episode to Claudia in 1975 on her return to Italy.

At that time, March 1975, Nicolina was staying with Claudia's family while her home was in the process of being renovated. One evening, when Nicolina was upstairs alone preparing for bed, out of nowhere her deceased grandfather appeared at the bedroom doorway. Nicolina, not believing her eyes, stared intently at the astonishing sight. She described him as having a look of shyness or embarrassment for interrupting her. Claudia and Nicolina's grandfather had died three years earlier.

Nicolina called out, "*Nonno?*" (This is "Grandfather" in Italian.) Then, just as quickly as he appeared, he disappeared. Nicolina swears she was wide-awake and not imagining it.

"No way was I sleeping, I was getting ready for bed," she vehemently declared. "I know what I saw, and I'll stand by it as long as I live."

Given the fact that Nicolina had stayed there for two weeks, I asked Claudia if her cousin had experienced any other strange phenomena. Claudia said, "No that was the only time Nicolina experienced something so bizarre."

In my opinion, I believe that the care and love Claudia and Nicolina's grandfather had for them has continued beyond our human limitations. Most of us believe in guardian angels, but what says that they have to be tall, blonde, perfect specimens? Why can they not be loving souls who at one time were a big part of our lives?

Who's Calling Me?

The next incident involving the house in Tagliacozzo happened to Aunt Valeria while she was vacationing there during the summer of 1993. My cousin Claudia has asked that I not approach my aunt on this subject, because, for some reason, it greatly upsets her.

One afternoon while Uncle Augie, Claudia's father, was outside keeping himself busy by mowing the lawn, my aunt, who was alone in the house, decided to sit in the living room and read her book. She had not been reading long when she clearly heard her name, "Valeria." The strange voice caught her attention. Once again, she heard her name called: "Valeria."

Thinking it was her husband, she answered back, "Augie, are you calling me?"

Not getting an answer, my aunt went to the window and saw my Uncle Augie on his lawn tractor, a good distance away, just putting along. Puzzled, but not too concerned, she sat back down and continued to read her book. What seemed like only a few minutes later, she heard her name again, but this time she recognized the voice: it was the voice of her father-in-law, Augie's dad and Claudia's *Nonno*.

Nervously, my aunt sat down, thinking it was just in her head. She was trying to go back to her reading when once again Nonno's voice called, "Valeria, Valeria!"

This time it seemed to come from directly in front of her. At this point, in order to get her mind away from the haunting voice, she abandoned her reading and headed off to the kitchen to prepare the evening dinner. Once out of the room, my aunt did not hear her name called again.

When my uncle came in from cutting the lawn, my aunt began to describe to him what she had heard. My uncle, being an extremely superstitious person and not comfortable listening or discussing anything concerning the paranormal, refused to listen to what my aunt experienced and changed the subject to other matters. As mentioned at the beginning of the story, even to this day, my aunt, so disturbed about the entire incident, refuses to talk about it.

Is it because she does not want to be ridiculed? Or is it that she does not want to believe that she heard from her deceased father-in-law?

Somebody Up There Loves You!

The next bizarre event at Tagliacozzo happened to my cousin Claudia while staying at the house in the summer of 2007.

Claudia was in the kitchen talking on the phone, and she had forgotten she had left a burner lit on the gas stove. Most Italian stoves have lids that cover the burners when not being used, and without realizing, she had closed the glass lid on the lit burner.

Claudia was only a couple of inches away from the stove when the glass lid exploded into a thousand pieces around her. The explosion was intense, but miraculously, she was not touched by even one piece of the sharp debris.

There she was, dazed, with dangerous glass shards all around her, and yet she was without a scratch! It was as if an invisible shield had protected her. Her boyfriend, Sal, hearing the explosion, came running into the kitchen and saw Claudia standing there, shaking and in shock. Sal, expecting to see Claudia critically injured or, even worse, killed, was amazed to find her unharmed.

Claudia swears she felt her nonno's presence during the horrific blast. She adamantly believes it was her nonno who protected her. It was as if he surrounded her with a protective barrier.

Claudia went on to tell me, "Right from the start, I have always felt something strange and different about our home in Italy. It doesn't scare me, it doesn't bother me, and, in fact, I love it. I never feel alone there. I welcome those experiences. I've always felt I've had a different awareness about people, places, and things, and I believe these events prove it." She added, "One last thing regarding my nonno. I was extremely close to him. When I said good-bye to him in the summer of 1971, I knew and he knew that I would never see him alive again."

Claudia went on, "As confirmation of my premonition, three months later, when we were back home in the United States, I dreamed he died; it was very vivid and real. I knew it was going to happen soon.

"I told my mother about it that morning and she brushed it off, stating, 'Italians believe that when you dream of someone's death, the opposite is supposed to occur, they wind up living a long life.'

"The dream stood in my mind all day; at school I couldn't concentrate on anything but my dream.

"The feeling of sadness that had engulfed me that morning would not leave. As we were sitting down to dinner that evening, the phone rang. Before my mother had a chance to pick it up, I instantly said, 'That's Italy.' It was, and it was my aunt in Italy telling us that Nonno was failing quickly and not expected to live out the night. I can assure you, I was not surprised that he didn't."

Didn't You Hear It?

Claudia experienced the following paranormal encounter at her home in Italy in the summer of 2008.

Claudia told me about an event that took place on a very quiet, sunny afternoon. Being such a beautiful day, she had decided to turn off the air conditioning, open all the windows, and enjoy the fresh air. Alone inside the house, she continued with her housework. Meanwhile, her boyfriend Sal was in the workroom out in the garage, finishing some leftover projects.

The next thing she noticed was Sal outside the bedroom window, looking in and asking her, "Do we have company?"

"No," Claudia answered. "Why are you asking?"

Sal told her that while he was in the garage, he heard a loud voice say "Claudia."

He said, "I heard a man's voice quite clearly and distinctly call your name in Italian, right next to me." He immediately walked the perimeter of the house and looked out onto the road, but there was no one to be seen.

Claudia asked Sal, "Did you recognize the voice?"

He said, "No."

Claudia truly believes it had to be either her deceased father or grandfather that Sal heard calling her. Since Sal had never heard either her father or grandfather's voice, there was no way of telling whom Sal heard, but Claudia insists that it was one of them, letting both Sal and Claudia know that they were still there for them.

Could it have been Claudia's father? Claudia told me that her father spent a lot of time in the workroom working on his projects. On the other hand, was it Claudia's nonno, again acting as her eternal guardian?

What Was That All About?

The last paranormal account concerning the house in Tagliacozzo has to do with a couple who rented the home in back 1976. The following is what they recounted to my cousin Claudia during her 2008 stay in Italy.

Claudia told me that her father (Uncle Augie) had to cancel their 1976 summer vacation to Italy because of business commitments. He thought that since they were not going, it might be a good idea to rent the house and have it occupied during their absence.

My uncle was fortunate to find a couple from South Africa, Ed and Joanna Richards, who signed a two-year lease. Ed was on assignment for an international company and wanted to rent a home near his work. My uncle's place fit the bill perfectly. Both Ed and Joanna were looking forward to making the house their home for the next two years.

Claudia had stayed in contact with Ed and Joanna through the years, and they continued to be good friends. During Claudia's 2008 trip to Italy, she decided to see if Joanna would like to meet for lunch.

However, Claudia had an ulterior motive in meeting with Joanna. It was just a few weeks earlier that Sal had had the strange experience hearing someone call Claudia's name. He and Claudia had searched the house and grounds for the source, but they came up empty-handed. With so many strange goings-on in the house, Claudia was curious to see if anyone from outside the family, like

Joanna and Ed, might have experienced anything peculiar during their stay.

Well, what Claudia was about to hear from Joanna would knock her for a loop. This is what Joanna told my cousin Claudia had happened one night back in 1976:

"We had been living in the house for about three months. One evening—which was no different from the others—Ed and I had dinner, talked about that day's events, watched some television, and around 11:00 p.m. started getting ready for bed."

[Claudia's note: This bedroom happened to be the same upstairs bedroom where one year earlier, March of 1975, Nicolina had seen our grandfather appear. Ed and Joanna knew nothing of that incident.]

"Ed was already in bed and starting to doze off. I was just getting into bed and about to put my head on the pillow when all of sudden I was lifted from the bed by some unseen force, spun in the air like a top, and violently dropped to the floor.

"Ed, sitting up in bed by then, witnessed the entire episode. Thoroughly shaken, I got up off the floor, and still in shock, I stared at Ed and said, 'What the hell was that all about?'

"Ed and I had no explanation for what happened; after the episode, we couldn't get back to sleep so we stayed up the entire night trying to figure out what the heck happened?

From what Claudia tells me, this was the only incident Ed and Joanna experienced while living in the home for two years.

What could have caused Joanna to literally be "flung" through the air so violently? Could it have been an earthquake? This region of Italy is known for its frequent earth tremors. Nevertheless, if it was, why didn't Ed experience it? After all, he was lying alongside her when it occurred. Or, was it Claudia's grandfather not liking the idea of having strangers living in the house?

My Wife, Lois, and Her Mother's Encounter with the Unknown

Sam Died but Never Left

While gathering materials for my book, I asked my darling wife Lois if she would mind if I included what she experienced with her mother when she was a teenager. Although a little hesitant at first, she finally agreed. I believe you will find this account bizarre to say the least. I know I did when I first heard it.

It was August 21, 1971, and a very warm, clear Saturday evening. Lois and her friend Marjorie had just finished dinner and were sitting on the wall in front of Lois's house, as they did on most summer nights. The wall was a popular gathering spot for the neighborhood teenagers during the summer.

On this particular evening, a car with four boys pulled up alongside of the wall. The girls, still sitting on the wall, peered into the vehicle to see who the boys were. The girls immediately recognized the kids as classmates from school. One of the boys, Sam Henry, was a neighborhood boy who lived just a few houses up the street.

Sam leaned out the car window and asked the girls if they would like to go to a party in Westport. He said they had left the rest of the gang there and were on their way to get some more beer.

Lois and Marjorie looked into the car and noticed that the driver of the car, who was also a schoolmate, shouldn't have been driving. He was only fifteen years old and was not even eligible for a learner's permit. The girls also noticed that the boys were holding open cans of beer. But what mostly concerned the girls was the slurring of words when the boys spoke. This was a definite giveaway to their condition.

The girls politely refused their offer; they were happy just to stay around the neighborhood. Not wanting their friend Sam to get into any trouble, the girls suggested that he stay with them, as the rest of the neighborhood gang would be there shortly. Sam and the rest of the boys just laughed. Wanting to get back to where the action was, the boys turned the volume back up on the car radio and took off.

News of the Horrible Crash

The next morning, Lois and Marjorie decided to walk over to Poplar Street, which was only a few blocks away, and hang out with some of their friends who lived there.

The girls made their way, walking on the cooler, shady side of the street and avoiding the hotter, sunny side. They could see a group of their friends already at the corner hangout, seeming unusually animated for this time of the morning. As Lois and Marjorie got closer to the group, they could hear their friends speaking excitedly to each other.

One of the kids turned to Lois and Marjorie and eagerly asked, "Did you hear what happened last night?"

The girls simultaneously answered, "No, what happened?"

The friend proceeded to tell the girls that there was a horrific car crash over on Pine Hill by the golf course. At two o'clock in the morning, a car with four kids was traveling at high speed, missed the curve, and crashed into a huge tree. All were killed except the owner of the car, who was not the driver but was seated in the back. Both of the girls were horrified to hear that one of the boys who did not survive was Sam Henry! Lois and Marjorie stood there in shock as the kids told them the gruesome details, making fun of the accident itself and the fact that Sam died. This group of kids had not been friends with that group of kids, and they proceeded to talk sarcastically about the accident.

The accident occurred around 2:00 a.m., on Pine Hill road. Even the people on Poplar Street, which was four blocks away, heard the crash. The people on Pine Hill went out to see what had happened. When they saw it was an automobile accident, they rushed over to help.

When they reached the vehicle, they could hear the boys desperately crying for help. The neighborhood people tried their best, using hammers, crowbars, and large pieces of wood to try to get the boys out, but it was to no avail. The only thing they could do was offer words of comfort and encouragement.

They told the boys that the police and fire rescue were on their way and told them to hang on.

As neighbors waited for what seemed for many that night to be an eternity, the voices coming from the vehicle became fewer and fainter. Finally, there was nothing but silence. The police and fire rescue arrived in just minutes. They worked feverishly using the jaws-of-life tool to pry through the twisted wreckage. It took the rescuers hours to remove the last victim. At the end, four of the five boys died at the scene. The only survivor was the owner of the vehicle, who was critically injured and was taken to Norwalk Hospital.

Still in shock about what happened, Lois and Marjorie tried to make sense of what they had just heard. One of the kids, whose father had tried to help the boys, said the police were going to tow the car to LaJoy's junkyard and have people view it. They wanted people to witness the results of drinking and driving, especially teenagers.

Lois's account does not describe a paranormal experience, but it is a prelude to what my mother-in-law, Dolores, told me regarding the Sam Henry tragedy.

A Deathly Experience

About a month after the accident, Sam Henry's Aunt Liz, who was a good friend of my mother-in-law Dolores, dropped by Dolores's for a visit. Dolores asked how Liz and her sister Bertha (Sam's mother) were coping with the tragedy.

Liz immediately started to cry and said, "Oh! Dolores, if I told you what happened, you probably would have my sister and I both committed to a mental hospital."

Dolores asked, "I don't understand, what's wrong?"

Liz went on to say, "Well, right after the accident, I stayed with Bertha for two weeks. Every day, Bertha would cry for hours. I was afraid to leave her alone, but I had to go back to work. I asked Bertha if she would be okay being alone. She said she would and told me that I should go back to work."

Liz hardly felt reassured but promised Bertha that she would call from work to check on her.

The next day, Liz went to work, and as promised, she called Bertha at lunch. Expecting to hear a depressed and exhausted person, you can imagine the shock Liz got when she heard a cheery, "Hello." It was as if the voice almost had a singing tone to it.

Liz asked if everything was okay and if Bertha wanted her to stop anywhere after work to pick her up anything. Bertha, again with a happy tone to her voice, said, "Oh no, 'we're' just fine."

Liz could not get over the sudden change in Bertha; it worried her. She also questioned the use of the word "we're" when Bertha was alone in the house. This went on for a few days: Liz would call, and Bertha would answer as happy as a lark with an "everything is fine here."

Liz decided to call a neighbor of Bertha's and ask if she had seen Bertha and if she seemed okay. The neighbor replied that Bertha was fine, and as strange as it may have sounded, Bertha's grieving had seemed to vanish overnight. Bertha's strange behavior concerned Liz, so she planned to drop by after work. Liz wanted to make sure Bertha was not having a mental breakdown.

Am I Losing My Mind Too?

Liz arrived at Bertha's around five thirty that afternoon. She rang the doorbell, hoping she would find Bertha in a good physical and mental state. Bertha answered the door with a great big "Hi" and gave Liz a hug and kiss. They walked into the kitchen where Bertha asked Liz to sit while she put on a pot of water for tea. As Bertha filled the teapot and walked over to the stove, Liz came right out and said, "I'm worried about you, Bertha, you know, being all alone here."

Bertha walked over to the kitchen table, sat directly across from Liz and said "Alone? What makes you think I am alone? Do you remember that night you left to go back to your house? Well, that same night I heard the front door open, and guess who it was? It was Sam! He gave me a big smile and went up to his room."

It was Liz's greatest fear: Bertha had been so badly traumatized by Sam's death that she was hallucinating and was surely on the threshold of a nervous breakdown.

As Bertha rose to prepare the tea, Liz tried to convince her of the truth by saying, "Sam is no longer with us, Bertha, and your grief is causing you to see these imaginary things."

Bertha, walking toward the kitchen table with both teacups in her hands, gave a smile and then slowly turned her head and looked toward the stairs. Liz, seeing Bertha looking intently at the stairs, also turned and looked. At this point, Liz could hear footsteps coming from the stairs. For a brief moment, Liz and Bertha looked at each other. Liz was startled at what she heard, but Bertha just continued to smile.

Once again, they turn their attention to the stairs. Liz thought that what she was hearing was probably someone who had come over to help Bertha pack Sam's things. The footsteps were getting louder, and Liz anxiously waited to see to whom the footsteps belonged to.

Liz first saw a pair of sneakers. As the sneakers started down to the next step, they led the way to blue jeans, which finally revealed a teenage boy—not just any teenage boy, but Sam! Liz glanced over to Bertha. Bertha, seeing Sam, smiled and continued placing the teacups on the kitchen table as though nothing was happening.

Liz, not believing her eyes, watched as Sam came down the stairs. Still looking straight ahead, he went over to the refrigerator and appeared to open the door. Liz could see that the door did not actually open, it just appeared that way. Sam stared at the shelf for a second, and then grabbed a bottle of Coke. To Liz, it looked as if he had taken a bottle out, but the actual bottle remained in the fridge. The bottle that Sam was holding was just as transparent as he appeared to her. Sam then closed the fridge door, and without acknowledging anyone, he turned and slowly walked up the stairs.

Liz's eyes were filled with uncontrollable tears, and not knowing what else to do, she grabbed Bertha, ran out the door, and drove to her house.

When Liz got home, she told their mother Rosie about what happened. Rosie, thinking that their daughters might have seen an intruder, told her husband, Walter, about the incident. All of them got into the car and drove back to Bertha's house. They searched everywhere, but couldn't find anyone.

After that incident, neither Liz nor Bertha ever saw Sam again. However, you can rest assured, whenever Liz visited Bertha, she always had someone with her. A few months later, Liz, with the help of the rest of the family, was able to convince Bertha that going to live with her daughter in Florida would be the best thing for her. Bertha, no longer seeing Sam around the house and having no other reason for staying in Norwalk, pretty much went along with the suggestion. In a short time, Bertha had sold the house and moved to Florida. As far as we know, Bertha never saw her son again.

When I asked my mother-in-law if Liz ever talked about the incident, she replied, "No, never again, and you can be sure that I never brought it up, either."

When confirming my mother-in-law's account with my wife, my wife went on to tell me that a few times, when driving past Sam's house late at night, she would look up and see a silhouette in the window of what used to be Sam's room. My wife would convince herself that what she saw was just her continued grief for her good friend and her sympathetic imagination.

Was it really just her sympathetic imagination?

Or, was it Sam, now unmercifully transformed into a tragic, proverbial restless spirit? Well, whatever it was, as soon as the new owners moved in, Lois never saw the silhouette again.

Do you think Sam moved to Florida with his mother? Or do you think he is still there in his family home—the only home he knew during his short life.

Part II

Paranormal Friends

Association

Steve Thomas ....fellow employee Stamford, Connecticut

Arnold Quassa ....fellow employee Stamford, Connecticut

Jerry Vassar ....high school friend Yonkers, New York

Ed and Helen Williams ....fellow employee Stamford, Connecticut

Veronica Treacher ....neighbor Oxford, Connecticut

Joan DiNapoli ....neighbor Oxford, Connecticut

Steve Thomas

The Jan and Thad Stacy Poltergeist Investigation

My good friend Steve Thomas lived in New York and worked with me in Connecticut. Knowing that I investigated the paranormal, he came up to me one day and asked, "Would you do me a great favor? I would like you to meet some friends of mine, Jan and Thad Stacy. They have been experiencing some strange noises and happenings in the home they just purchased, and from what they tell me, it sounds like it could be something paranormal."

I asked Steve, "What makes you think what they are experiencing is paranormal?"

Steve replied, "Frank, I was over to their house this past weekend. We heard what I thought were footsteps coming from the upstairs bedroom, which is right above the dining room where we were sitting. When my friends and I went upstairs to check, we could not find anything out of the ordinary. However, while we were upstairs we heard what sounded like the front door slamming shut! My friends told me that this kind of stuff has been happening since they moved in two weeks ago. You need to see this for yourself. I am at a loss on what to do next. These weird goings-on are way over my head, but I think they would be right up your alley. I told my friends that I would mention this to you and see if you would be able to stop over and, hopefully, help them resolve this problem."

I told Steve that the earliest I could go would probably be Saturday. I asked him to call his friends and see if that would be a good day to have us come by. Steve immediately grabbed the phone in my office and called his friends. His friends, without skipping a beat, agreed. In fact, they tried to get me to come over that evening, but Vails Gate, New York, was just a little too far for an evening jaunt from Connecticut. So the plan was for me to be at Steve's house on Saturday afternoon, leave my car there, and go with him to his friends' home.

The Road Trip

Saturday morning arrived, and the sky was a bright blue. There was a distinct chill in the air left over from the previous night, but I could see the sun making its way over the pines that lined the backyard. After lunch, I said good-bye to my wife Lois, got in my vehicle, headed down the driveway, and started on my road trip to Vails Gate, New York.

Vails Gate was about seventy miles north of New York City and a little over an hour from where I lived in Connecticut. While motoring my way west, I was going over in my mind the research I did prior to my trip. I had been amazed at what I had discovered. Vails Gate and the adjacent area of the southern Hudson River Valley have an extensive presence in early American history, beginning in the late 1600s, when the Dutch settlers first came to the area, and continuing into the Revolutionary War period. What really excited me was during the war for independence, the town of West Point, where the military academy now resides, was a strategic location for the Colonists. Many skirmishes were fought in that area between the Patriots and British soldiers and where many of them unfortunately met an untimely death. It didn't surprise me that people could be experiencing paranormal activity.

Meeting the Home Owners

It was a short drive to Jan and Thad's house. Passing through the hamlet of Vails Gate, you sensed the deep history that engulfed its narrow streets. It was easy for me to imagine what it must have been like living here one hundred or even two hundred years ago. After leaving Vails Gate, we had traveled about two miles on Blooming Grove Turnpike when Steve suddenly pulled his car into a driveway. For some reason, I pictured the house on a secluded dirt road outside of town, not off a main thoroughfare. However, there it stood, on a lot between two newer homes and across the street from a strip mall that included a hardware store, cleaner, deli, and bakery. The eighteenth-century house was definitely out of place with its surroundings. Steve and I walked up to what looked like the original front door to the home and rang the doorbell.

After a quick introduction, Steve's friends, Thad and Jan, led us to the living room. Jan brought out some coffee and pastries, which she jokingly bragged were freshly baked every morning at 3:00 a.m., at the bakery across the street door. I, being a pastry freak, could smell them as soon as I walked into the house, and I was hoping we would be offered some.

I started the conversation by asking, "So, Steve tells me you have been experiencing some very strange things. Can you elaborate on this for me?"

Thad said, "It started the first night we moved in. Just before going to bed, I was in the kitchen, and I noticed the door going down to the cellar was open. I know that I had bolted it closed not more than fifteen minutes before. I asked Jan if she had opened it, and she answered, 'No!'

"Thinking nothing of it, Jan and I stopped our moving-in process and went to bed. Around 1:00 a.m., we both heard what we thought were men laughing and making a commotion; it was coming from the living room. Cautiously, I got up and went downstairs to see what was going on. I switched on the lights and there was no one there. Jan had made her way down the stairs too. We looked at each other in wonderment as if to say, 'What the hell is going on here?'"

Looking into the History of the Home

Thad went on to tell me that this had been happening on and off for about a week. Trying to get down to the cause of the disturbances, Thad called the real estate agent and asked if he knew if the former owners had similar experiences. Moreover, were these experiences the cause of them selling the home? Thad was told that the house was used as rental property and the owners did not live there. The agent also found out that the last tenants had moved out after only living there for two months. Thad was also told that the renters before them had lived in the house for just six months before packing up and leaving without notifying the owner.

Thad asked the real estate agent if he knew of any strange occurrences associated with the home. The agent was not aware of any problems with the house. Perhaps he did not want to to reveal any problems, fearing a lawsuit from Thad and Jan. Thad went on to tell us he found out that in New York state there is a "Housing Law," which states if you believe your home is haunted, it needs to be on the seller's disclaimer statement. But as suspected, there was no disclaimer in their contract.

At this point, Jan took over, "One day, while Thad was at work, I went to the local historical society where I was able to find an amazing story associated with our home."

What Jan found out was that the home was originally built in 1755 as a tavern and was a major stop for the stagecoach that traveled from Trenton, New Jersey, to Albany, New York.

She also discovered that at the start of the Revolutionary War, because of their loyalty to the colonists' cause, the tavern owners were captured by the local Indians, who sided with the British, and they were given to a company of Hessian soldiers. The Hessians locked the tavern owners in one of the rooms and made the tavern their headquarters. Reading further, Jan found out that a few nights later, while Hessians were partaking in their nightly drinking party, colonist militia from the nearby village of New Windsor surprised them.

During the ensuing engagement, the colonists killed ten of the German mercenaries and took the rest as prisoners. The tavern was given back to the original owners. In 1805, the tavern was sold and made into a private home. It remained a private home and with the same family until 1933. It was then sold to a local doctor, whose family kept it as a rental property until Thad and Jan purchased it.

Having the history of the home, Thad and Jan gave us a tour. Other than the ceilings being slightly lower than you would find in most homes, the home was in great shape and very charming. After the tour, we decided to have an early dinner. I suggested we go to the Bear Mountain Inn. It had been a long time since I had been there, and I was anxious to see if it had changed. Everyone agreed, so off we went.

At dinner, we discussed at length what we would do as part of the night's investigation. We formulated a plan, which included EVP (Electronic Voice Phenomena) sessions where we would try to capture voices and sounds that normally cannot be heard by the human ear. We also would take photographs using my high-speed, high-resolution camera. In addition, we would use the video recorder to capture any activity that was in progress.

After dinner, Steve took us for a short walking tour of Vails Gate. Vails Gate turned out to be a charming little town, a place where you would not mind living and raising a family.

The Investigation Begins

We got back to the house and readied ourselves for the night's adventure. We waited until about 12:00 a.m. to start our investigation. According to Thad, that was when most of the activity started.

Just like clockwork, at midnight we heard rumbling coming from across the hall. The sound was coming from the room Thad and Jan used as their home office. We all walked in together, and to our surprise, we saw all the desk drawers were open. Before we started, we had done a thorough inspection of the house, and I recalled that all of the drawers to the desk had been closed. At no time had anyone in the group been walking around on their own.

As we were discussing what could have caused the drawers to be pulled open, we heard a commotion directly above us in one of the bedrooms. We immediately ran up the stairs and into the bedroom. There, in a little alcove in the wall to our left, was a bureau with clothes lying on top; one of its drawers was open. When we had checked the rooms upstairs earlier, everything was in its place and there were no clothes left out anywhere.

The next incident did not occur until a little after three o'clock in the morning. Steve and I were in one of the spare bedrooms, doing some EVP work and taking photographs, when we heard what sounded like men arguing and glasses breaking. We rushed downstairs to see what was going on. Thad and Jan, in the kitchen videotaping, had also heard the racket and were running toward the parlor—the room they thought it came from. Expecting to see a group of home invaders and a room severely trashed, we saw and found nothing. There was no damage, and no person or persons were in the room—not one thing was out of place. We searched diligently, looking for any type of evidence that could have caused the commotion, but we could not find anything.

After that event, we did not hear or see anything for the rest of the night. Around five o'clock, Steve and I decided to wrap things up and head for home. I told Thad and Jan that I would get back to them as soon as I had a chance to listen to the tapes, review the photographs and video, and further research the property's history.

The following Monday during lunch, Steve and I called the historical society. The first thing we did was validate the information Jan had told us. The historical society, being very gracious in helping with our request, confirmed everything Jan had said regarding the home's history.

Follow-up and Analysis

On Tuesday at lunch, Steve and I checked with the US Geological Survey (USGS) in Weston, Virginia, to see if there were any earthquakes that evening in the Vails Gate area. In addition, we asked if they could tell us what type of rock was the most common in the area, as crystal, granite, and limestone are said to have properties that are conducive to creating paranormal environments. Lastly, we checked whether they knew of any underground streams running under the location of Thad and Jan's home since rivers and streams are also known to create paranormal environments.

It was not until Thursday that I heard back from the US Geological Survey on our inquiries. They told us the following information:

> There were no earthquakes in the area during the timeframe we had asked them to check on.

> The rocks most common in the area are: Quartz, Pyroxene, Biotitic, Magnetite Garnet, Calcite, Dolomite, Gneiss and Granite.

> As for streams or rivers, the closest water system noted was an underground stream that was located approximately 125 yards northeast of the address of the home.

I thanked them for getting back to us so quickly and for their help. I then called Steve and asked him to stop by at lunch so we could go over the findings.

At lunch, I took out the notes from the conversation I had had with the USGS. I told Steve that they had no reports of seismic activity in the area for that day. As for the geology being the cause of the paranormal activity, I mentioned to Steve that we could dismiss this also, since the known culprits (certain types of stone) were not present. Finally, the possibility of the aquatic aspect being a factor was dismissed because of the distance of known water systems from the home—they were too far away to be causing any of the paranormal activity.

With all the natural causes rejected, we looked to see if a train might have happened by during our investigation and caused the commotion. Looking at a topographical map of the area, the closest train line was located on the western side of the Hudson River, about five miles east from the home.

Then we thought it might have been a large eighteen-wheeled truck, but Steve brought to my attention that several trucks had passed by while we were setting up for our investigation, and they were barely noticed. I asked Steve if he would please finish his review of the voice and video tapes when he got home that night, and I would analyze photographs. I wanted to have all our findings packaged and ready for Jan and Thad's review on Saturday.

The next day at lunch, Steve reported his findings to me. After listening to three hours of audio tapes, he was astonished that we did not pick up any of the sounds we had heard. Not even the loud crash and glass breaking we all had heard coming from the dining room. I stated to Steve that after reviewing the seventy-two photographs that were taken that night, I was not able find one abnormality.

The Reveal of Our Research

On Saturday, Steve and I went back to present Jan and Thad with our evidence—or lack of it. When Jan and Thad heard we did not have anything for them to listen to or see, they were puzzled. They could not comprehend how we were not able to capture any of the activity from that evening.

Thad anxiously asked, "Did we all hear the racket that night, or was it just our imaginations?"

I tried to explain to them, "This kind of thing happens frequently. You think you have finally captured what is undeniable proof of paranormal activity. However, when you review your evidence, there's nothing there."

Jan and Thad sat there, shaking their heads in disbelief, mentioning that just last night they both heard what sounded to them like people arguing in a foreign language, perhaps German, coming from the basement.

Thad said, "I got up from the couch, went into the kitchen, and opened the door to the basement. As soon as I turned on the light, the arguing stopped cold. With the activity still occurring, what are we supposed to do next?"

Both Steve and I, feeling helpless, did not know how to answer Thad.

After a moment, I suggested to Jan and Thad that they have a psychic medium come to their home and see if he or she could determine if there were spirits residing in their home and, if so, how they might be freed from their imprisonment. With that, I gave them the names and telephone numbers of a couple that were experts in hauntings and psychic investigations.

I said confidently, "I'm sure they will be able to help you with this matter."

Thad and Jan thanked both Steve and me for our help in trying to resolve their paranormal problems. Before leaving, I remembered something I found out while researching the area's history.

I asked Thad, "Are you originally from this area?"

He answered, "Yes. In fact, I was told by my grandfather that our family has lived in this area for hundreds of years."

I then told Thad about my research of the area. In my investigation, I came across the name "Moodna Creek." The name *Moodna* is slang for "Murders" in Dutch. Folklore had it that some time back in the late seventeenth century, a family by the name of Stacy had had a homestead along the creek. One day, a neighbor, who had not seen any of the Stacys for a number of days, went to their homestead. There he found that eight out of the ten family members had been massacred. The only survivors were two small boys about four or five years old. For years people tried to find out from the boys what had happened, but were never able to get them to talk about it. The doctors concluded that the boys were so traumatized that the event was totally erased from their memories.

I said to Thad, "That's something you might want to look into in your spare time. Perhaps in some strange way, this might be a factor in what you and Jan are experiencing in your home."

The Update

One Monday morning, about six months later, for some reason I had the Stacys on my mind. I called Steve and asked how Jan and Thad were doing and if they were still experiencing any strange occurrences.

Steve said, "It's funny that you are asking about Jan and Thad. I forgot to tell you they had put the house up for sale about a month ago and finally sold it this past Saturday."

I asked Steve, "Did they finally get rid of the problem they were having?"

Steve replied, "To tell you the truth, I hadn't been there or talked to them for almost three months, since you and I were there. Then about a month ago, I got a call from Thad telling me that he and Jan planned to put the house on the market. For some unknown reason I did not even mention anything about the activity they had been experiencing. It just didn't cross my mind at the time. Speaking with them this past Saturday, they told me they sold the house and were planning to leave the state. Again, neither they nor I mentioned anything about what happened. However, I'll ask them the next time I speak to them."

I said, "Don't! Let's leave well enough alone."

Well, I never did find out if Jan and Thad had taken care of the supernatural problem. I hope that if they didn't, they at least had the courtesy to mention it to the new owners: "Oh! By the way, the house you just purchased, well, it's haunted."

Arnold (Doc) Quassa

My Friend, the Witch Doctor!

Back in the early 1980s, Arnold Quassa and I both worked in Stamford, Connecticut. Even though Arnold lived in Brooklyn, New York, we often went fishing and crabbing on our days off. After his retirement, Arnold moved back to the West Indies and we somehow lost touch, but I will always remember him as being one of my best friends.

With Arnold being from West Indies and me having an Italian heritage we spent many a lunchtime talking about each other's customs and family ancestries. It was during one of these lunch discussions that we happened to be talking about another favorite topic of ours, the paranormal. That's when Arnold told me that his father had been a well-known shaman in the West Indies.

Arnold asked, "Do you know what a shaman is?"

When I answered, "Yes, and I'm also familiar with Caribbean taboo history," it really surprised him.

He then asked, "Do you believe it?"

I answered, "No, I think it's just some old superstition that scares everyone in the West Indies."

He answered, "So you do, do you! Okay, let me tell you about something my father did years ago to a troublemaker who lived on our island, and then you can decide."

Arnold proceeded to tell me of an incident concerning an evil person who lived in their town on an island in the West Indies. This person was known for always causing trouble, badgering and beating people and forcing them to give him their money. I guess he would be our equivalent of the "town bully."

You Don't Fool with the Shaman

One day, Arnold and his father were walking through town when this evil person sped through the town square, went through the stop sign, and hit a little girl who was crossing the street. Luckily, the little girl was not hurt seriously. Witnessing this, Arnold's father decided he had had enough of this evil person's antics. He proceeded to walk toward the man and his vehicle, all the time mumbling ritual prayers. As he stood directly in front of the man, Arnold's father raised his arms and shouted out some commands in an ancient African language, causing the evil person to fly out of his car. The evil person got up off the ground and started to shake uncontrollably. Screaming in pain, he fell to the ground and getting up on all fours, he ran into the woods like a wild dog.

The next day, word had spread through the town that the evil person had packed his belongings and moved to another part of the island. Arnold went on to say, "I was only nine years old when this took place, but I remember it as perfectly as if it had happened yesterday."

I asked Arnold, "Where did your father get those powers? Do you have any of his abilities?"

Arnold answered, "I have some powers; they are nothing like my father's, but I still can do, as you say, some strange things."

I said, "Like what, for instance?"

His reply was, "I can travel out of my body." I guess Arnold saw the doubting expression on my face because he immediately said, "I will prove it to you; I will travel to your house this evening and report back to you tomorrow on what you were doing at the time of my visit."

In true disbelief, I said to Arnold, "If you can do this, I will buy lunch for the rest of the week." He said nothing, but gave me the same smile the Cheshire cat had in *Alice in Wonderland*.

The Journey to Norwalk

The next morning, I got to work a little early. I was anxious to hear what Arnold had to say and, to my surprise, Arnold was already there. We got ourselves a cup of coffee and took a couple of seats in the employee's lounge.

"Well, my doctor (as in witch doctor), what do you have to tell me?" I asked.

Arnold began by saying, "At around 10:00 p.m., I went into my living room and sat in my favorite chair. It took me a while to get comfortable and place myself in a spiritual receptive state. However, in a short time, I started to feel myself slowly slipping out of my physical body and rising toward the ceiling, all the time watching "me" still sitting in the chair below. The next thing I knew, I was out of my apartment and rushing through the night sky over Brooklyn."

He then explained that at first he seemed disoriented, but then he was able to concentrate and direct himself toward Norwalk, Connecticut, where I lived. I don't know how he did this because at that time, Arnold had never been to my house or, for that matter, even knew where Norwalk, Connecticut was!

Then he said, "Before I knew it, I found myself over your house. I knew this was your house because I recognized your SUV in the driveway."

The next thing he did was scan my living room and he proceeded to describe how it was laid out. He depicted the type of chairs and tables, and said that I had two sofas.

He also described my kitchen and said my wife was preparing her lunch for the next day. And most impressive was when he told me that I was watching a football game, and the score on the screen was 10 to 7 in favor of the New York Giants with one minute and twenty-five seconds to halftime!

What Are You Doing with a Cannonball?

In addition, to prove he had visited me, he said, "I did something last night, which you found to be very strange this morning." He then asked, "Did you notice something peculiarly out of place when you left for work this morning?"

With a smirk I answered, "Yes, but I want you to tell me what it was!"

Arnold proceeded to say, "I moved a cannonball. Yes, a cannonball. By the way, what you are doing with a cannonball? Anyway, I moved it from the front porch of the house to the bottom of your apartment stairs at the back of the house."

I was totally shocked; he was right. The Civil War cannonball, a keepsake of the family who owned the home, was always kept on the front porch by the door. However, this morning, for some unexplainable reason, it was at the bottom of my stairs at the back of the house!

I was speechless and frozen with goose bumps. From that day on, I stopped calling him Arnold and started calling him Doc.

By the way, as I promised, I did buy Doc lunch for the rest of the week.

Jerry Vassar

Near-Death Experience (NDE)...
What it feels like to Die

Brothers Jerry and Phil Vassar attended the same high school that I did, and they were good friends of mine. Phil was a fellow classmate, and we both majored in electrical wiring; Jerry majored in carpentry. Since Jerry's lunch period coincided with ours, he usually sat and ate with us. I will now recount an experience Jerry had that changed his outlook about life at the young age of twelve.

Why Are You So Afraid of the Water?

It was my junior year in high school, and spring had finally arrived. While we were at lunch one day, a few of us were talking about joining the swim team. We thought it would be a great way to get out of classes, and it would be fun to visit the other high schools in the county and see how their schools compared to ours. You see, our school had been an old boiler factory once, and it had no pool. We had to walk about four blocks and use the nasty, dirty pool at Public Bath House No. 6 for swimming practice.

We all laughed and agreed it would be a fun to do. That is, all of us except Jerry Vassar. Jerry quickly jumped in and said, "Not me, I came too close to 'buying the farm' a few years back, and I don't want to go through that strange experience ever again!"

Well, that's all he had to say to get my attention. It was just about this time in my life that I started getting interested in UFOs and the paranormal. So I asked, "What do mean you don't want to

81

go through that strange experience again? What happened?" Then Jerry proceeded to tell us about his experience, with his brother Phil nervously listening in.

What It Feels Like to Die!

Jerry went on to say that it happened when he was twelve. It was a hot summer day in August, and he, Phil, and a few of their friends decided to go swimming at Tibbetts Brook Park, the Yonkers, New York town pool. Phil, being a year older than Jerry, was a more experienced swimmer, but Jerry was confident that he could hold his own with the rest of the gang. Jerry watched in envy as the bigger kids had a great time going off the diving board.

Wanting to experience that fun, Jerry waited until Phil and the other kids jumped in and started swimming toward the lower end of the pool. Jerry then climbed the ladder and with one big run, he jumped off the board. Jerry quickly realized that this end of the pool was way over his head. He tried searching for the bottom of the pool with his feet, but it was to no avail. He was not able to touch the bottom to spring back to the top. He started to panic.

Jerry, making a windmill motion with his arms, was showing us how he tried desperately to swim to the top. But despite his efforts, he had found himself sinking slowly downward and swallowing water.

Streaking through This Tunnel of Light,

It was just about this time that Jerry started to experience a strange and eerie silence around him. He said in amazement, "All of a sudden, I could see myself lying at the bottom of the pool, feeling no pain or fear."

Then, with a sudden jolt from behind, he found himself rising very fast through the water, watching his lifeless form at the bottom of the pool disappearing very quickly. It appeared to Jerry that he was rushing through the blackness of outer space and heading toward what he thought was a bright star. As he got closer, the star looked more like a tunnel with a bright light at its entrance.

As he streaked through this tunnel of light, he saw ahead what appeared to him to be the end of it. Once out of the tunnel, Jerry stood in the midst of what he could only describe as the most beautiful light he had ever seen. From this point, he could see fields upon fields of the most colorful flowers one could ever imagine.

The next thing he recalled was a person whom he thought was a man, but he wasn't quite sure. The figure was tall, with long blond hair and a flowing white robe. The only thing he could surmise was that the figure was an "angel." While all this was happening, Jerry had noticed he was no longer anxious or frightened. In fact, he felt euphoric. He was so happy to be where he was.

Out of nowhere, Jerry heard a voice, but he could not tell where it was coming from. He looked over at the angel and noticed he was smiling, but the voice was definitely not coming from him.

He Saw His Life Displayed before Him

The voice was telling Jerry to observe the cloud above him, and in a split second, there appeared the whitest cloud against the most beautiful blue sky he had ever seen. The cloud then proceeded to develop into what seemed to be a giant movie screen. As Jerry stared at the cloud or movie screen, he saw every event he had experienced during his short life on earth. He saw birthdays, Christmases, his first day at school, and even the time when he was five years old that he hit his brother Phil with a rock, causing Phil to have ten stitches.

He said, "I felt that I was Phil at the moment I hit him with the rock. I even felt the pain that Phil had felt." It was as if he was watching a 3-D movie of his entire life right in front of him.

He then was shown what Jerry believed was his future. He saw himself married and having children, and he saw what he believed was himself as an old man with grandchildren.

Jerry then heard the same voice say, "Jerry, you need to go back now. Your brother is crying and urgently calling you. As you can see, there is so much for you to do, and so many people are depending on you for this to occur."

As soon as the unknown voice was finished, Jerry once again found himself hurling through the tunnel and flying through the black void of space. During his travel back, Jerry was upset and confused; he did not want to leave the angel or the fantastic place. However, what Jerry wanted was not to be, at least not yet.

Back to Life Again

From above, he could see himself approaching the pool. As he got closer, he noticed a crowd around a boy lying on the concrete by the pool. There were EMT people working frantically on him. Jerry, hovering right above the action, could see Phil crying and calling to this boy. When Jerry looked at the boy, he could see that *he* was the person that the EMTs were trying to revive!

Then, *Bang!* With a terrific jolt, the next thing Jerry knew, he was coughing up what he felt was the entire pool. With that, the EMTs breathed a sigh of relief, placed Jerry in an ambulance, and sent him to the hospital where he stayed overnight for observation.

Well, to say the least, all of us were speechless. We looked over to Jerry's brother Phil for confirmation as to what Jerry had just finished telling us. Phil quietly nodded his head and said, "That's just the way it happened."

Being nosey, I asked Jerry, "Do you happen to know how long you were *dead*?"

Jerry answered, "From the time they pulled me from the water to the time I started breathing, the EMT told me it was about fifteen minutes."

Again, looking to satisfy my curiosity, I asked Jerry, "What do you think about the experience you had? Do you think you might have been imagining this?"

Jerry's reply was, "I might have, but it seemed too real for that. The person I called the 'angel,' well, I always feel like he's around, especially when I'm getting myself in some kind of awkward situation."

Jerry continued, "You can take it for what it's worth, but everything I told you is the truth. I know for sure that there's definitely something after this life, and I experienced it."

After hearing about Jerry's adventure, we thought it would be a good idea *not* to join the swim team that year.

Ed and Helen Williams

Ouija Board Incident . . . It's Not a Kids' Game

This narrative is for everyone who likes to play with Ouija boards. I, too, enjoyed dabbling with the cardboard specter until this one night, which changed my relationship with this sinister amusement.

This takes place in Norwalk, Connecticut, back in 1978. It involves Ed and Helen Williams, my wife Lois, and me. Ed and I had worked together for over four years; we had an excellent working relationship and enjoyed talking about old comedy movies.

One morning before work, Ed stopped by my cubical, inquired about my involvement in the paranormal, and asked if I was still investigating and researching cases. I was quite surprised, because in the four years I had known Ed, he had never mentioned my parapsychology work.

I answered, "Yes, when time allows, I assist a senior parapsychologist with cases that occur in the New York and New England areas."

That's when he asked if I would do him the greatest favor and come over to his house to see if I could help his wife, who was having a terrible time with voices and recurring, realistic nightmares.

I told him, "Ed, perhaps it would be more beneficial if she sought professional help, you know, from a doctor or psychologist."

He replied, "My wife spoke to her best friend about this problem. Her friend suggested that before she sees a psychiatrist, I should seek out someone who has experience in interpreting dreams, like a medium or psychic. That's when I thought of you."

I asked, "I'm not a medium or a psychic. How am I supposed to help?"

Ed answered, "Her friend believes that using an Ouija board might help. I have heard you talk about having used one, so that's what brought me to you. Please, Frank, I'm desperate."

I felt bad for Ed; I had never seen him so serious. I said "Okay," and I agreed to come over Friday night to see if I could help. Ed thanked me and went back to his work, relieved.

He Can Burn in Hell for Eternity

The following Friday night, Lois and I went over to Ed's house. After casual introductions, Helen, Ed's wife, brought us into the living room where she started to describe her experiences. Helen began by saying, "It started about two weeks ago when I received a phone call from my sister in Vermont saying that our father had passed away; she asked if Ed and I planned to attend the funeral."

Helen had answered her sister by saying, "Never! And for all I care, he can burn in hell for eternity."

Helen went on to tell us how she despised her father for the way he had treated her mother and the rest of the family. In fact, she blamed him for causing her mother to die before her time. Helen went on to say, "He was a drunkard and abusive person. He would beat my mother and us kids regularly, that's why I hate him." Helen, now with tears in her eyes, continued, "My mother passed away when I was sixteen. I vowed that as soon as I turned eighteen, I would leave Vermont and go to live with my favorite aunt in Connecticut."

Seeing how upset Helen was, I asked, "How can I help?"

"It's about the dreams I'm having," Helen whispered. "It started the night of my sister's phone call. In my dream, I was sitting at the kitchen table at my old house in Vermont; my father came in, and with his hands together in a begging gesture, he said, 'Please, my little girl, forgive me for what I did to you and the family, please?' I remember that in my dream that I cursed him and said, 'You deserve to rot where you are, and furthermore, never, ever bother any of us again—never!' The next night I had the same dream, but my father seemed to be in more agony than before. Again, I cursed him and screamed for him to get out of my life. I did this so loudly that I woke Ed."

Helen paused and clasped her hands over her face in sheer exhaustion. She regained her composure and continued by stating that this traumatic experience had now taken a turn for the worst. Helen claimed she now saw her father's ghostly image and heard his pleas even during the day, and she could not take it any longer.

At this point, Ed and Helen looked at me for an answer.

I said to them, "There's no doubt your dad is trying to contact you. I'm not a medium, and to try to get one tonight would be impossible. However, what I can do if you are willing? We can try using the Ouija board, but I can't guarantee that it will work."

Helen, being desperate, was willing to try anything. I went to my car, got the board, and set it on the coffee table.

Messages from Beyond

I told them that Ed would not be a good partner for the reading because he, being married and close to Helen, might influence the direction of the *planchette* or pointer. Therefore, I asked my wife to "partner" with Helen for the reading. I could see from the expression on her face that my wife did not like that idea. She hates anything having to do with the paranormal and believes it is nothing but evil. However, being a caring person, and seeing how upset Helen was, she was willing to help in any way she could.

My wife and Helen placed their fingers on the planchette and asked the following questions:

"Is there anyone here with us tonight?"

The planchette moved to *Yes* and then spelled out *Dad*.

"What do you want?"

The planchette spelled out *"Forgiveness"* and continued to spell out *"I cannot move on without it."*

Helen then asked, "Why should I forgive you?"

The planchette spelled out, *"Because everyone else has, even your mother; I cannot join her until you do."*

At this point Helen was crying profusely. I could see that my wife was also getting upset. As for Ed, well, he did not know what to do.

Helen looked at me and asked, "Should I?"

I answered, "Yes."

I explained, "On the 'other side,' there is nothing but love, and all hate is forgiven. You need to forgive and love also."

We all stared at Helen, anxiously waiting for her response. She answered, "I forgive you, Dad. And Dad, I love you."

Immediately after Helen said this, the planchette went on to spell out, *"Thank you . . . Love always . . . Dad,"* and then it spelled out, *"and Mom . . . Good-bye."*

Don't Touch It! It Could Be Something Evil

We all looked at each other, somewhat shocked but relieved. You could feel the air in the room change. The heaviness that my wife and I felt when we first walked into their home was no longer there. Everything seemed brighter and cheerful. In addition, there was a noticeable change in Helen's presence. Her tired, bloodshot, and darkened eyes seemed to have disappeared, and her face was happy and glowing. We proceeded to the dining room for some coffee and my favorite, homemade blueberry pie.

While we were sitting having coffee and pie and discussing the night's events, I noticed Helen anxiously looking past me toward the living room.

As the rest of us turned to see what she was looking at, Ed shouted, "Look, the planchette! It's moving on its own!"

Helen immediately got up to take hold of it. I jumped up and stopped her just as she was about to grab it.

Curiously, she asked, "What's wrong, why did you do that? It might have been my mother trying to contact me."

I explained to her, "Your father said 'Good-bye,' and he is no longer here among us. Whatever was moving that planchette and trying to come through could not have been anything good. This is a very common way in which evil entities enter our realm."

I did not mean to frighten everyone, but I had learned from my research and other case studies that once the planchette says "Good-bye," it is over! At that point, I packed up the Ouija board. The unexpected episode gave us a great scare. Nervously, we went back to the dining room and finished our coffee in total silence.

I did not hear from Ed or Helen the rest of the weekend, so when Monday morning came, I was very anxious to see how things were going. Around 8:00 a.m. Ed stopped by my cubical. He wanted to thank Lois and me for all we had done for him and especially for Helen. He added that everything at home seemed even better than before; things were more peaceful and very pleasant.

As for the Ouija board, well, the next morning after visiting Ed and Helen, the first thing I did was to go to my car and take out the Ouija board. I walked around the backyard, looking for a good place to dig a two-foot hole. I found a great spot by the side of the garage. I dug the hole and placed the Ouija board in it. Then I took some gasoline and lit the board. Once it had burned to just ashes, I buried it. Since that episode, I refuse to touch another Ouija board. Case closed!

Veronica Treacher

The Ghost Boy from the Lake

In 1994, when we lived in Connecticut, a neighbor of ours reported this very bizarre account to me, which, at the least, I think you will find incredibly strange.

We had been living in our new home for a few months, and it dawned on me that we did not really know all of our neighbors. Therefore, I thought it would be a good idea to have a get-together with everyone so we could to come to know each other better.

We were all having a great time. At one point during the party, my wife asked me if I would please get her another cup of coffee.

I was in the kitchen pouring her a cup, when Veronica Treacher, who was one of our neighbors, came in and asked, "Is it true that you investigate paranormal phenomena?"

"Yes," I said. "How do you know that?" I added curiously.

She answered, "Joan told me," referring to another neighbor.

Veronica asked if could relate an incident that occurred to her and her brother when they were kids. She went on to say that she and her brother had never told anyone but their parents about it, but they always felt the need to talk to someone who could understand what they went through. She asked if I would please listen and tell her if she and her brother were just imagining things. Here is what Veronica related to me that night.

This occurred when Veronica was twelve years old and her brother was ten. Their father had been transferred from his office in Bergen County, New Jersey, to an office in Fairfield, Connecticut. She remembered her father and mother rushing in after spending the day house hunting in Connecticut as if were yesterday. Smiling brightly, they announced they had found a very nice home on a lake in Trumbull, Connecticut, just a few miles from his new office.

Veronica and her brother were very excited and could not wait for summer to come so that they would be able to go swimming, fishing, and boating, and have fun living by the lake. The whole family was thrilled and could not wait to move.

Hide and Seek

In just a couple of months, the family had moved into their wonderful dream house by the lake. It was winter, and they were spending the first Saturday in their new home. Both Veronica and her brother could not wait to go out in the snow and explore their new surroundings. After telling their parents they were going out to play, they headed toward the lake; their mother called out to them, telling them to be sure to not go close to the ice. Both kids acknowledged their mother's instructions and marched through the snow to explore their backyard.

As they were making a snowman, Veronica's brother noticed a boy hiding behind a group of trees. He shouted over to Veronica and said, "Veronica, there's a boy hiding by the trees."

Veronica said, "Let's see if he wants to play with us."

Veronica and her brother started over to the group of trees where the boy was hiding. The boy playfully laughed and kept dodging behind the trees. Veronica and her brother ran to the tree where the boy was hiding, but couldn't find him. Then they saw him pop out from behind a different tree. They called to him to stop hiding so they all could play together. Nevertheless, the boy was always a few steps ahead of them and kept popping out from behind a different tree just as they would get close. Veronica was frustrated and told her brother to forget about trying to catch up with him. Veronica, shivering, suggested they go home, get some hot chocolate, and warm up.

As they turned to go home, Veronica's brother dropped one of his mittens. As he bent down to pick it up, he noticed something that was very strange. He said to Veronica, "Hey, Veronica, doesn't it seem weird that we don't see any footprints in the snow where the boy was? And another thing, why wasn't he wearing a coat? It's freezing out here."

At this point, Veronica did not pay much attention to what her brother was saying; she just wanted to get out of the cold, get her hot chocolate, and watch her favorite Saturday morning cartoons.

While Veronica and her brother were having their hot chocolate, Veronica told her mother about the boy they saw in the backyard.

Their mother asked, "Do you think he lives in the big yellow house up the road?" Both Veronica and her brother shrugged their shoulders as if to say, "I don't know."

They went on to tell their mother that every time they tried to catch up with the boy, he would disappear from behind the tree where they thought he was hiding and then all of a sudden pop out from behind a different tree.

Veronica asked her mother if it would be okay if they went up the road to the big yellow house to see if the boy lived there.

Their mother answered, "That's fine, but I want you both home by three o'clock." With their mother watching, Veronica and her brother put on their snow clothes and headed up the road.

The Nice Lady

Tracking through the knee-deep snow made for a laborious hike to the neighbor's house. Occasionally they looked up to see how much farther they had to trek. It seemed to take forever for them to get there. Finally, there, Veronica reached up and rang the doorbell.

The door opened and an elderly woman, looked down at the kids, smiled, and asked, "Hello, children, what can I do for you?"

Veronica introduced both her and her brother and told the woman that they had just moved into the red house down the road, and they were her new neighbors.

The woman said, "Why, that's wonderful; I was wondering who bought that lovely home."

The woman asked if they would like to come in and have some cookies that she had just finished baking for her grandchildren. Veronica and her brother couldn't resist the offer, especially after getting a whiff of the mouth-watering aroma coming from inside the woman's home.

While having the cookies, Veronica asked the woman if her grandchildren were staying with her. The woman answered, "No, but they are coming for lunch tomorrow. If you'd like, you and your brother are welcome to stop by and meet them."

Then Veronica asked, "Are there any other kids who live close by?" The woman answered, "No, all the kids around here have grown up. There are no children your ages."

Again, Veronica asked, "Are you sure? Just this morning, my brother and I saw a boy playing in our backyard. We thought he might have lived here or close by."

The woman smiled and said, "Oh, I'm pretty sure the only children around here are my grandchildren when they visit." With that, the woman served Veronica and her brother more goodies and continued with small talk.

That's the Boy We Saw

After having their cookies and milk and enjoying each other's company, Veronica looked up at the clock and saw it was almost 3:00 p.m. and time to head home. Thanking the woman for the cookies and milk, Veronica and her brother started putting on their coats and boots. Veronica's brother, while wrestling with his coat, was studying a photograph on the bookcase, and suddenly he shouted out, "Hey, here's the boy we saw!"

Veronica, looking closely at the photo, chimed in, "Yeah, that's him!"

The woman took hold of the framed photograph and said, pointing to the boy in the photo, "You mean this boy next to my granddaughter?"

They both answered simultaneously, "Yes, him!"

The woman, possessing the most surprised and sorrowful look, said, "Oh no, honey, that couldn't be him." The woman hesitated, not knowing whether she should continue to explain. She took both Veronica and her brother's hands gently and, softly speaking, continued her account. "You see, just last summer, this boy and his family was living in the same house you now live in. One day, when there was no one was around, he somehow managed to untie his father's rowboat and took it out on the lake.

"About an hour later, his mother, not seeing him in his room playing with his toys where she had seen him last, became nervous and started looking for him. She searched all over the house, upstairs, downstairs, and the attic; he was nowhere to be found. She searched the backyard and looked for him in the tool shed; again, he was nowhere to be seen. She then came here and asked if I had seen him. I said, 'No,' and I helped in searching for him.

"Looking out to the lake, our greatest fear came to light. We saw the rowboat floating out on the lake with no one in it. She immediately called the police. By the afternoon there were over fifty people here on the lake, helping to look for him. They searched the rest of the day and into the night. This went on for three days, but they never did find the boy."

Veronica and her brother, totally shocked and scared out of their wits, looked at each other, thanked the woman for the cookies, and headed for home as fast as they could. Both were anxious to tell their mother the story they had just heard from the woman. Once home, they called to their mother, had her sit on the couch, and proceeded to tell their story.

After recounting the incident, Veronica and her brother eagerly waited to see what their mother's reaction would be. To their surprise, their mother just laughed and said, "The lady was playing with you; it's probably just a joke!"

Veronica went on to tell me, "After that day, we didn't see the boy any more. A few days later, at school, I asked the kids if they had heard about the accident. They all said it was true, and it did happen. One kid, who knew the boy, told me that his parents still had a copy of the newspaper article that reported the accident. They kept it because they were friends of the boy's parents."

The Accident Did Happen

Veronica asked if she could borrow the newspaper article so she could show her parents, and she promised that she would return it the next day. The boy agreed and the following day gave Veronica the newspaper article.

"I took the newspaper article home to show my parents. When they read it, they just looked at each other in disbelief. At first, they did not know what to say, but then they apologized to my brother and me for not believing us. From then on, they always believed what we told them. We lived in Trumbull for three more years before my father was transferred back to New Jersey. But during those three years, my brother and I had many sleepless nights thinking about that boy in the backyard."

What Veronica had just related to me was astonishing, even for someone like me, who thought I had heard it all. Yes, I have been told of similar instances, but this was the first time I had heard it directly from the person who experienced it.

Veronica went on to say, "I hope you believe me. If you don't, you can call my brother, and he will validate all of what I said. Even to this day, whenever my brother and I talk about it, we get freaked out."

Did I believe Veronica? Well, let's put it this way, I didn't find any reason not to believe her. We were neighbors for five years, and I always found her and her husband to be of excellent character and good friends. I stressed to Veronica that by no means was she the first or would she be the last person to experience such phenomena.

In fact, it could even happen to you!

Joan DiNapoli

Alien Encounter

There is one more account that I would like to include regarding UFOs. This incident took place in Oxford, Connecticut, and happened to a neighbor of ours. It may not be as dramatic as my brother's UFO experiences, but when it was told to me, the excitement it caused my neighbor could still be heard in her voice.

You might recall I spoke of a "get-to-know-you party" we had for our neighbors when we first moved to Oxford, Connecticut, in 1991. Joan and Tim DiNapoli, a couple who lived just around the corner from us, were also invited to the party. Their daughter, Mary, often played with our daughter, Nicole. So we thought it would be nice to get to know them better.

Just as Veronica had followed me into the kitchen to tell me of her and her brother's experience with the "ghost boy," Joan followed me when I went to fill up a couple of trays with crackers and cheese. As I reached up to grab the box of crackers, I heard Joan ask if I had a minute. She wanted to discuss something that had happen to her the previous fall that had made a major impact on her religious beliefs—and she was trying to find out how to understand what she had experienced.

I asked, "Why are you asking me? Shouldn't you speak to Tim about things like this?"

Joan answered, "No, I know he wouldn't understand if I told him. He would either laugh at me or tell me it was just my imagination, or both!"

Joan continued to say, "The word in the neighborhood has it that you deal with the paranormal, and I'm sure what I've experienced falls in that category. Please hear me out?"

Seeing Joan was serious and quite upset, I said that I would, I just needed to take the trays out, and then I would be right back to listen to her story.

Guess Who's Coming to Dinner?

On my return, Joan and I sat at the kitchen table as she recounted what had happened one evening the previous fall.

Joan started with, "It had been a spectacular New England fall day. The sun was warm and the cloudless sky was the prettiest robin-egg blue you'd ever seen. It was about 5:00 p.m., and I was starting to get the ingredients together for our evening dinner. Tim had called earlier to let me know he was still in Hartford and would try to get home by 6:30 p.m., so I had plenty of time to prepare.

I hadn't heard Mary for a while, so I peeked into her room to make sure everything was okay; she was doing her homework. Seeing that everything was fine, I returned to the kitchen to continue with the dinner preparations.

"I walked over to the pantry, took out the macaroni pot, and brought it over to the sink to fill it with water. I was gazing out the kitchen window, admiring the beautiful sunset, when I noticed what I thought was the headlight of a small plane coming toward me. I didn't pay any special attention to the bright light; Oxford airport is only a few miles to the east of where we live, and the airport's flight path takes the planes right over our home.

"I placed the pot of water on the stove, lit the burner, and went to the fridge to get the ingredients to make the salad. Passing by the kitchen window, I noticed that the light had become brighter and bigger. Again, thinking it was just a small plane flying lower than usual, I thought nothing of it. I brought the vegetables over to the sink and began to wash them. Glancing up and looking out the kitchen window, I realized there were a couple of things that were very odd about this approaching airplane. It was traveling very slowly, and most of all, there was no sound of a motor! Then it dawned on me: it was probably a helicopter. The Sikorsky helicopter complex was about ten miles down the valley; it had to be one of their vehicles.

"But helicopters are usually ten times louder than the small planes, especially in the valley where the sound becomes boxed in between the mountains. I checked to see if the window were closed, this would explain me not hearing the sound of the engines. I reached to touch the glass. To my surprise, I touched the screen—the window was wide-open.

"Now I was starting to get worried. Perhaps the plane had lost power and was about to crash. I started to reach for the wall phone to call 911 when the bright light went completely out. It was as if someone had a switch and just flipped it off. I placed the phone back on the receiver and headed toward the window to get a closer look. Focusing intently on where I saw the light last, I thought I was seeing something, but it was hard to tell with the kitchen lights on. I went over to the doorway and turned the kitchen lights off. I still couldn't tell what I was looking at, so I walked through the dining room, opened the sliding doors to the deck, and went out to get a better look.

What the Heck Is This Thing

"Out on the deck, I scanned the backyard and looked toward the pond, which is located on the farm next door. I was straining my eyes to see through evening darkness. It was at this point that I noticed a silhouette against the starry sky. There was definitely something out there because the silhouette was blocking some of the stars. I said out loud, 'What the heck is that thing?' From where I was standing on the deck, the pond was about two hundred feet away. The thing I was staring at was maybe another fifty feet from the shore, not quite in the middle of the pond. Whatever it was, it was not making a sound, and it just stayed about ten feet above the pond in dead silence.

"Then, in an instant, the object lit up, casting a bright light across the pond and the adjacent fields. I was shocked; I could finally distinguish the shape of the object. It was a classic 'flying saucer,' dome and all! Just as fast as I recognized it to be a flying saucer, that's how fast I ran back into the house.

"For whatever reason, and to this day I don't know why, I turned off the lights in the kitchen and crouched down behind the kitchen island. I was scared out of my wits. Crouched down behind the island, I could hear Mary in her room, singing away while doing her homework; she was not aware of what was going on outside. Not wanting to frighten her, I kept the incident to myself and let Mary keep singing away in her room.

"Still on my knees, I worked my way over to the sink. I slowly raised my head just above the sink and peeked out the window. Damn! It was still out there. However, it was no longer as bright as it was. In fact, the object seemed to be pulsating. The light would first dim and then brighten in a rhythmical pattern. From what I could tell, the object was about sixty to seventy feet long and ten to twelve feet high with a dome in the middle. It also had placed some kind of pipe or tube into the pond and seemed to be drawing water from the pond. Feeling a little braver, I stood up and watched what was going on.

"Four or five minutes must have gone by when I noticed a car's headlights approaching from Laborde Road. I was excited that someone else would finally observe this UFO. I stood there, anxious to see what the person in the approaching car would do. Would the person stop and look? Or speed up and run for the hills?

"I was nervously watching both the UFO and the approaching car, when all of a sudden, the UFO disappeared. I could not believe what happened—the darn thing was gone! I watched as the approaching car slowly drove by as though nothing was there and everything was normal.

I Was Watching Them as They Were Watching Me!

"As soon as the car made the left turn on to Pisgah Road, the UFO reappeared. Again, it was as if someone had turned on a light switch. As for the pipe or tube that was siphoning the water, it was no longer extending from the bottom of the craft. For some unknown reason, I was no longer frightened by my encounter. As strange as it may seem, I felt that the experience was something positive. I was still staring out the window in amazement when I noticed along the rim of the craft what appeared to be a row of windows. Then, silhouetted against the windows, were what appeared to be three small beings looking toward me! However, I wasn't frightened; I was watching them as they were watching me. Then from below, at its center the craft flashed a light. This was repeated three more times; I got the feeling that the entities on the craft were acknowledging my presence.

"All of sudden, I had the urge to have Mary share my experience. I called to Mary, telling to her come to the kitchen quickly. I heard her opening her door and running toward the kitchen.

"A fraction of second before Mary entered the kitchen; the object sort of wobbled and then shot up, disappearing into the evening sky. Mary came running into the kitchen and asked, 'Why did you call me, Mom?' I turned and looked sadly out the window where just a second ago the object had been hovering. I turned back toward Mary and not knowing what to say, I simply asked, 'Do you want spaghetti or butterfly macaroni for dinner?' Mary answered, 'Spaghetti is fine.'"

With that, Joan told me she continued preparing dinner while rerunning the extraordinary events of that evening through her mind.

Joan's experience had raised my curiosity, so I started my questioning:

- "At any time did you ever feel threatened?"
  Joan answered, "When I first went out on the deck. But once I was back in the house, the longer I watched, the less worried I became."

- I asked, "How long did this entire episode last?"

  Joan replied, "About twenty minutes. After Mary left the kitchen, I looked up at the clock and it was about 5:20 p.m. The water for the macaroni had almost completely boiled out of the pot. I had to replace about a half a pot of water."

- Then I asked, "You mean to tell me you never told Tim about this?"

  She replied, "No, Tim does not believe in this kind of stuff. If I mentioned to him what had happened, he would have thought I was ready for the funny farm!"

- My next question was this: "How about yourself? Did you believe in UFOs and the paranormal before this incident?"

  Joan replied, "I always believed we are not the only living beings in the entire universe, but I never believed in UFOs, ghosts, Big Foot, or any of that stuff. I still don't. That is, except for UFOs. I'm now a believer!"

- My last question: "Did you ever see a UFO after that incident?"

  Joan answered, "No, but there have been some nights that I would wake up and sense something telling me to look out the window, but I never did. I felt if I did, I would be starting something that would probably haunt me forever."

Then Joan asked me, "What do you think I saw? Was I imagining it? Was I daydreaming, or did it really happen?"

I fired right back with, "What do you think?"

She took a deep breath and said, "I guess I'm one of the people who other people go around saying are crazy."

My reply to that was, "You have joined the ranks of millions of people who have had similar experiences. And my guess is that in the coming years, those ranks will grow astronomically. Perhaps one day soon you will be able to say, 'I was one of a few people who saw an entity before it became an acceptable occurrence.'"

With that, Joan and I went back into the living room and joined the others.

Joan has never approached me about the subject again. Perhaps she was afraid of the ridicule that comes with the territory, or it may be that she just wants to forget the whole thing. Whatever it is, I did respect her privacy.

Conclusion

I hope you have enjoyed *Paranormal Family and Friends* and found it to be what you were looking for regarding the paranormal.

My objective was to provide you with accounts that were bizarre, eerie, and fascinating. *Paranormal Family and Friends* was also intended to help substantiate the activities associated with supernatural occurrences. By utilizing events that happened to my relatives and close friends, I have removed the concerns of fabrications and hoaxes.

Paranormal Family and Friends was not intended to be used as a text or as reference on the subject of the supernatural but as an assemblage of baffling experiences that fellow paranormal followers and people who are curious about the paranormal would find amusing and weirdly interesting.

As I have mentioned, I was quite surprised to find out that so many paranormal incidents had occurred within my family and to my close friends. After years of investigations, research, and travel, who would have known that the best cases were right on my doorstep?

Finally, I propose this challenge to my fellow paranormal colleagues: go and ask your family and friends if they have experienced an incident that could be termed paranormal. Even if they say they haven't, I'll bet they know or knew of someone who has!